First World War
and Army of Occupation
War Diary
France, Belgium and Germany

41 DIVISION
124 Infantry Brigade
Queen's (Royal West Surrey Regiment)
10th Battalion
5 May 1916 - 31 October 1917

WO95/2643/1

The Naval & Military Press Ltd
www.nmarchive.com
Published in association with The National Archives

Published by

The Naval & Military Press Ltd

Unit 10 Ridgewood Industrial Park,

Uckfield, East Sussex,

TN22 5QE England

Tel: +44 (0) 1825 749494

www.naval-military-press.com

www.nmarchive.com

This diary has been reprinted in facsimile from the original. Any imperfections are inevitably reproduced and the quality may fall short of modern type and cartographic standards.

© Crown Copyright
Images reproduced by permission of The National Archives, London, England, 2015.

Contents

Document type	Place/Title	Date From	Date To
Heading	WO95/2643 (1)		
Heading	41st Division 124th Infy Bde 10th Bn Q.R. West Surreys May 1916-Oct 1917 Mar 1918-1919 Jan In Italy 1917 Nov-1918 Feb		
War Diary	Aldershot	05/05/1916	05/05/1916
War Diary	Southampton	05/05/1916	05/05/1916
War Diary	Le Havre	06/05/1916	07/05/1916
War Diary	Steenbecque	08/05/1916	08/05/1916
War Diary	Outtersteen	09/05/1916	29/05/1916
War Diary	Steenwerck	30/05/1916	30/05/1916
War Diary	Ploegsteert	31/05/1916	03/06/1916
War Diary	Trenches	04/06/1916	23/06/1916
War Diary	Billets	24/06/1916	30/06/1916
Miscellaneous	124 I.B. K. 389/C.F. 10.d.	17/06/1916	17/06/1916
Miscellaneous	Ref. 124/I.B.-389 C.F. 10d.-16/6/16	18/06/1916	18/06/1916
Miscellaneous	Programme for Smoke and Shrapnel		
Miscellaneous	C Form (Original). Messages And Signals.	20/06/1916	20/06/1916
Miscellaneous	A Form. Messages And Signals.	20/06/1916	20/06/1916
Miscellaneous	Appendix 2		
War Diary	Trenches 103-112	01/07/1916	05/07/1916
War Diary	Billets	06/07/1916	10/07/1916
War Diary	Trenches.	11/07/1916	17/07/1916
War Diary	Papot	18/07/1916	22/07/1916
War Diary	Trenches.	23/07/1916	31/07/1916
Miscellaneous	Officer Commanding, 10th. Bn. "Queens" R.W.S. Regt.	12/07/1916	12/07/1916
Miscellaneous	124 I.B.	13/07/1916	13/07/1916
Operation(al) Order(s)	124th. Infantry Brigade, Order No. 29	13/07/1916	13/07/1916
Operation(al) Order(s)	124th. Infantry Brigade, Order No. 35	19/07/1916	19/07/1916
Miscellaneous	Time-Table Of Operations.		
Miscellaneous	Appendix 3		
Miscellaneous	O.C. 10th Queens.	26/07/1916	26/07/1916
Miscellaneous	Appendix 5		
Operation(al) Order(s)	124th Infantry Brigade Orders No. 28.	12/07/1916	12/07/1916
Operation(al) Order(s)	124th Infantry Brigade Order No. 38	24/07/1916	24/07/1916
Miscellaneous	124th Infantry Brigade.		
Map			
Miscellaneous	Messages in Connections Mish Raid	26/07/1916	26/07/1916
Map	Sector Raided Enclosed In Blue.		
War Diary	Trenches	01/08/1916	02/08/1916
War Diary	Soyer Farm	03/08/1916	03/08/1916
War Diary	Rest Billets.	04/08/1916	10/08/1916
War Diary	Trenches	11/08/1916	16/08/1916
War Diary	Soyer Farm.	17/08/1916	17/08/1916
War Diary	Noote Boom	18/08/1916	23/08/1916
War Diary	Buigny l'Abbe.	24/08/1916	07/09/1916
War Diary	Camp	08/09/1916	14/09/1916
War Diary	Trenches	14/09/1916	19/09/1916
War Diary	Bivouac	20/09/1916	30/09/1916

Miscellaneous	Nominal Roll Of Officers, N.C.O's And Men-Killed, Wounded And Missing Of 15th, 16th, And 17th Sept. 1916	19/09/1916	19/09/1916
Miscellaneous	B Company		
War Diary	In The Field	01/10/1916	31/10/1916
War Diary	Ridge Wood	01/11/1916	03/11/1916
War Diary	Trenches	04/11/1916	09/11/1916
War Diary	La Clytte	10/11/1916	14/11/1916
War Diary	Right Sector Trenches	15/11/1916	21/11/1916
War Diary	Ridge Wood	22/11/1916	26/11/1916
War Diary	Trenches N 18.10-07-1	27/11/1916	30/11/1916
War Diary	Mun? Trenches	01/12/1916	01/12/1916
War Diary	La Clytte	03/12/1916	06/12/1916
War Diary	Trenches	07/12/1916	13/12/1916
War Diary	Ridge Wood	15/12/1916	31/12/1916
War Diary	La Clytte	01/01/1917	01/01/1917
War Diary	Trenches	02/01/1917	08/01/1917
War Diary	Ridgewood.	09/01/1917	14/01/1917
War Diary	Trenches.	15/01/1917	20/01/1917
War Diary	La Clytte	21/01/1917	25/01/1917
War Diary	Trenches.	26/01/1917	31/01/1917
War Diary	Ridgewood	01/02/1917	04/02/1917
War Diary	Trenches	05/02/1917	10/02/1917
War Diary	Steenvoorde	11/02/1917	23/02/1917
War Diary	Merrembrige Camp	24/02/1917	27/02/1917
War Diary	Trenches	28/02/1917	28/02/1917
War Diary	Trenches	01/03/1917	06/03/1917
War Diary	La Clytte	07/03/1917	11/03/1917
War Diary	Trenches	15/03/1917	18/03/1917
War Diary	Ridgewood	19/03/1917	21/03/1917
War Diary	Steenvoorde	22/03/1917	06/04/1917
War Diary	Reninghelst	07/04/1917	12/04/1917
War Diary	Trenches	13/04/1917	19/04/1917
War Diary	Chippewa Camp	20/04/1917	30/04/1917
War Diary	Trenches	01/05/1917	03/05/1917
War Diary	Chippewa Camp.	04/05/1917	18/05/1917
War Diary	Bayenghem	19/05/1917	31/05/1917
War Diary	Middle Camp East	01/06/1917	04/06/1917
War Diary	Trenches	05/06/1917	30/06/1917
Miscellaneous	Headquarters, 124th. Infantry Brigade.	10/06/1917	10/06/1917
Miscellaneous	Operation Order by Major R.V. Gwynne. D.S.O.	20/06/1917	20/06/1917
War Diary	Meteren	01/07/1917	17/07/1917
War Diary	Vestoutre	18/07/1917	24/07/1917
War Diary	La Clytte	25/07/1917	25/07/1917
War Diary	De Zon Camp.	26/07/1917	31/07/1917
War Diary	Trenches	01/08/1917	06/08/1917
War Diary	H 36 C 34	07/08/1917	07/08/1917
War Diary	H 36 35 C 7.4	08/08/1917	10/08/1917
War Diary	Trenches	11/08/1917	15/08/1917
War Diary	Thieushoek	16/08/1917	24/08/1917
War Diary	Staple	25/08/1917	25/08/1917
War Diary	St Martins Au Laert	26/08/1917	31/08/1917
War Diary	St. Martins Au-Laert Billets.	01/09/1917	15/09/1917
War Diary	St Marie Capelle	16/09/1917	16/09/1917
War Diary	Thieushouk	17/09/1917	17/09/1917
War Diary	Ridge Wood	18/09/1917	23/09/1917

War Diary	Pradelles	24/09/1917	27/09/1917
War Diary	Chyvelde	28/09/1917	30/09/1917
War Diary	Ghyvelde.	01/10/1917	22/10/1917
War Diary	Ghyvelde.	06/10/1917	10/10/1917
War Diary	Iwkirve Farm	11/10/1917	15/10/1917
War Diary	Dunkirk	16/10/1917	31/10/1917

2/24/91
2pm (back)

3/25/91
9am (front)

41ST DIVISION
124TH INFY BDE

10TH BN Q.R.WEST SURREYS

MAY 1916 - ~~DEC 1918~~ OCT 1917
MAR 1918 - 1919 JAN

(IN ITALY 1917 NOV - 1918 FEB)

To 123 BDE.

QN 226 — SECRET

2nd / 4 / XLI — 10 West Surrey V₂ᴬ

WAR DIARY or INTELLIGENCE SUMMARY
Army Form C. 2118

Place	Date	Hour	Summary of Events and Information	Remarks and references to Appendices
Aldershot	5/76	9 am	The Battn. left Aldershot (3 Train loads) for Port of Embarkation.	H.
Southampton	—	7 pm	Embarked and sailed for Le Havre.	H.
Le Havre	6/76	6 am	Disembarked and marched to Dock Rest Camp. 2 Lts Brown, Bird, Barr & Erickson to Boom.	H.
	7/76	5 am	The Bn. (less "A" Coy Capt Beadell) entrained for EBBLINGHEM	H.
	—	5.30 pm	"A" Coy entrained	H.
Steenbecque Ebblinghem	8/76	4 am	Detrained and marched to EBBLINGHEM (less A Coy)	H.
	—	2 pm	" " " " A Coy	H.
			when the Battn. went into Billets. Cold showers - good roads.	
Oultersteen	9/76	9 am	marched to the Area OULKERSTEEN and went into Billets. Showery - good roads.	H.
	10/76	—	Billets - Bayonet fighting, musketry, Phy. training etc.	H.
	11/76	—	" " Practice with Gas helmet - in Gas attack.	H.
	12	—	" " Coys went for a route march - 13 miles.	H.

Army Form C. 2118

WAR DIARY
or
INTELLIGENCE SUMMARY
(Erase heading not required.)

Place	Date	Hour	Summary of Events and Information	Remarks and references to Appendices
Outtersteen	13"		Billets - Outtersteen. "	
Outtersteen	14"		Billets "	
Outtersteen	15"		Billets "	
"	16		" "	
"	17		" "	
"	18		" "	
"	19		" "	
"	20		" "	
"	21		" "	
"	22		" "	
"	23		" "	
"	24		" "	
"	25		" "	
"	26		" "	
"	27		" "	
"	28		" "	
"	29		" "	

WAR DIARY
or
INTELLIGENCE SUMMARY

Army Form C. 2118

Place	Date	Hour	Summary of Events and Information	Remarks and references to Appendices
Steenwerck	30/5	8 p.m.	In billets – marched from Ouderdom to Steenwerck A.	
Oasphort	31/5	7 a.m.	" " " Steenwerck A. (Div. Reserve)	

To Officer i/c
O.C. Office
Boo

Morley
Lieut Colonel
Commdg 10 Queens

Vol 2
Army Form C. 2118.

WAR DIARY
or
INTELLIGENCE SUMMARY
(Erase heading not required.)

XY

10 W Surrey
Ff

Place	Date	Hour	Summary of Events and Information	Remarks and references to Appendices
PLOEG STEERT	6/76	—	In Reserve billets. No 6/10322 Pte A.J. BROWETT and 6/10224 Pte H.E. YOULL wounded by shrapnel when working improving the trenches near Regimental work. Pl.	
"	9/76	—	In Reserve billets. The following were wounded by shell fire:- No 9779 Pte P.D. McCULLOCH; 6/10179 G.T. B WILLS, 6/10136 Pt W.H. BATES; 9/9502 F.J. KENYON; 6/9995 Pt T. MILLAR, 9/6160 Pt C.S. DAWES, 9/9571 Pte GREENFIELD; 6/6387 Pte SPEAIGHT; 9/7740 Pte H. GLEADLES all at MAISON 1675. 6/9491 J.H. CAMPBELL at DELENNELLE - Pl.	
"	8/76	—	In reserve billets Pl. 11/2	
Yencho at 1/76	—	moved into trenches No 10316 Ptc Regiment. 6/8513 Pte A. FARR wounded by sniper Pl.	
"	5/76	—	Yencho Pl.	
"	6/76	—	" " Pl.	
"	7/76	—	In trenches - the following were killed wounded - Killed	

Army Form C. 2118

WAR DIARY
or
INTELLIGENCE SUMMARY
(Erase heading not required.)

Instructions regarding War Diaries and Intelligence Summaries are contained in F. S. Regs., Part II. and the Staff Manual respectively. Title Pages will be prepared in manuscript.

Place	Date	Hour	Summary of Events and Information	Remarks and references to Appendices
Trenches	7/6	—	Killed 9/6946 Pte TRES ONH: Wounded L/11133 Pte E. ECKERSLEY; L.C.(95) 9/10340 (?) TRUETT, J; 7301 Pte E.H. PHILO; L/11227 Pte E. ROGERS, 9/10187 Pte A.W. JONES, 9/10210 Lcpl & BARKER; 9/10264 Pte C.A. MELLETT. AL	
-"-	8/6	—	Trenches - no casualties AL	
-"-	9/6	—	Killed 9/9430 Sergt. J. LENNARD, 9/10017 Lcpl S.J. MOORE; AL	
-"-	10	—	-"- AL	
-"-	11	—	Trenches - quiet AL	
-"-	12	—	Reserve trenches AL	
-"-	13	—	-"- -"- AL	
-"-	14	—	-"- -"- AL	
-"-	15	—	-"- -"- AL	
-"-	16	—	-"- -"- AL	
-"-	17	—	Trenches 103 to 112 AL	
-"-	18	—	-"- 103 to 112 AL over	

Army Form C. 2118

WAR DIARY
or
INTELLIGENCE SUMMARY
(Erase heading not required.)

Place	Date	Hour	Summary of Events and Information	Remarks and references to Appendices
Trenches	18/6/16	—	Continued — Wounded Captain J. T. BRETHERTON; Lieut F. R. HOGGETT; No 6985 Pte H. CRITCHER; 10175 Pte A. TAYLOR; 9867 Pte C. GOAD. One was let off in the enemy line about 11.40 P.m. but owing to the trouble went on. Blowing it was drifted back over the German line M.	appx (1)
-"-	19th	—	In the trenches M.	appx 3 appx (2)
-"-	20th	—	In the trenches M.	See attached (1) M.
-"-	21st	—	Trenches — Killed no 9837 L.Cpl S. MORRIS, 10170 Pte H. SPENCE; Wounded — 9873 Cpl S. P. CLARKE. M.	appx 2 M.
-"-	22d	—	Trenches — Wounded 9771 Pte F. F. SHADDICK; 769 Pte E. POWELL. Killed no 9946 Pte R. J. W. GREEN; Wounded Sergt R. FRETWELL, 9933 291	
-"-	23d	—	2Lt. L. E. ANDREWS, 5/9469 Sergt. R. FRETWELL, Pte R. FRY M.	
Trenches Billets	24th	—	C. RODLEY, 10045 Pte R. FRY Billets — Wounded 6891 Pte KENTON. W.C. M.	

WAR DIARY
or
INTELLIGENCE SUMMARY
(Erase heading not required.)

Army Form C. 2118

Place	Date	Hour	Summary of Events and Information	Remarks and references to Appendices
Billet	25	—	Continued	
			Quiet – Wounded 6/6815 Private S. FAULKNER M.	
"	26	—	Wounded with working parties no 7712 P S BELSHAM S.T; 5/10367	
			Private H BLOUT M.	
"	27	—	Billets M.	
"	28	—	" " — Accidentally wounded no 6810 P T.N. PALMER M.	
"	29	—	" " — Died of wounds no 9423 P J. GREENWAY - wounded	
			no 9/10093 Sergt S. HARDING; 5/10004 Sergt T.J. HOWITT, 5/9847	
			Cpl A. BEECH, 5/10109 L-Cpl F.W. BRADSHAW, 6/4925 P G. LEE,	
			6/10310 P E. TAYLOR: M.	
"	30	—	Billets – Killed 6/10239 P F. SMITH M.	
			Trenches occupied 103-11Z - Bde on our right 123rd Inf Bde on left 2/KRR	
			In the Field	
			30/6/16	

R. Oakley Lieut. Colonel.
Commdg. 10 Queens

SECRET.
124 I.B.
K.389/C.F.10 d.

The Divisional Commander wishes to have smoke discharged and to treat the opposing trenches with shrapnel on 4 occasions before the 24th.inst.,commencing on Monday 19th.inst.,in accordance with the attached programme, the object being by using smoke to induce the enemy to man his parapets, and then inflict loss on him by means of shrapnel.

The smoke should not be discharged unless the wind is from W. to S.W., and not less than 5 miles per hour, or more than 8 miles per hour (the first implies a steady breeze, the latter a fresh wind)

45 minutes before the time named, Battalions will notify Brigade Headquarters that weather conditions are favourable.

30 minutes before the operations should commence, the artillery and troops detailed to throw smoke bombs will be warned by wire from Brigade Headquarters, by a pre-arranged signal, as to whether the operation will take place or not.

Retaliation is to be expected.

O.C.Battalions must take the necessary precautions with regard to working parties and troops in trenches being under cover.

An indent has been submitted for drawing necessary number of smoke bombs and smoke candles.
When these are available Units concerned will be informed, and will be held responsible for drawing same from D.A.C.Dump and transporting them to our front line.
They are on no account to be issued until required.

Major,
Brigade Major,
124th.Infantry Brigade.

17/6/16.

SECRET.   Copy No. 1

Ref.124/I.B. - 389 C.F.10d.-16/6/16.

1. The dates fixed for the operations detailed in the above letter are as follows:-

        Operations   P....19th.June
                            Q....20th.June
                            R....21st.June

2. If the wind is unfavourable on any of the above dates, the operation arranged for that date will not take place but will be cancelled entirely.

3. The following code words will be used by battalions in notifying Brigade Headquarters whether weather conditions are favourable, and by Brigade Headquarters in ordering whether operations will or will not take place.

Date	Battalions to Brigade.		Brigade to Battalions & R.F.A.	
	Weather conditions favourable	Weather conditions unfavourable	Operations will take place.	Operations will not take place.
19th.June	DOG	CAT	CIGARETTES	TEETOTAL
20th. "	PIG	SHEEP	BAROMETER RISING	BAROMETER FALLING
21st. "	COW	HORSE	FRESH MEAT	BULLY BEEF.

4. If the 124th.Infantry Brigade is relieved on the 21st.June operation "R" will not take place.

5. Artillery do not require withdrawal of men from Front Line Trenches. O.C.Battalions will exercise their own discretion as to the withdrawal of men having regard to (1) the number of men normally occupying front line Trenches(2) the number of bombers introduced into front line trenches for the operations.

6. Officers in charge of Working Parties will be instructed to get their Working Parties under cover in case of retaliation.

                                                       Major,
                                                 Brigade Major,
18/6/16.   124th.Infantry Brigade.
Issued at

                Copy No.1 10th.Bn."Queens"
                  "   2 26th.Bn.R.Fusiliers.
                  "   3 32nd.Bn.R.Fusiliers.
                  "   4 21st.Bn.K.R.R.C.
                  "   5 237th.Fd.Co.R.E.
                  "   6 228th.Fd.Co.R.E.
                  "   7 122nd.Inf.Bde.
                  "   8 123rd.Inf.Bde.
                  "   9 187th.Bde.R.F.A.
                  "   10 190th.Bde.R.F.A.
                  "   11 17th.Inf.Bde.

PROGRAMME OF SMOKE AND BOMB ATTACKS.

Date	Letter of Operation and Unit carrying it out.	Wind	Frontage on which smoke to be discharged.	Duration of discharge of smoke From / To		Arty. to open fire on enemy's trenches opposite & 100 yds. to either flank, From / To		REMARKS.
1st.Day Monday 19th.inst.	P 32nd.Bn.Royal Fusiliers	W. to S.W.	Whole of trench 125 (270x front) 100 smoke bombs.50 Payne Candles	5 pm.	5.4pm.	5.2 pm.	5.4 pm.	124th.Infantry Brigade to inform 123rd. I.Bde. of dates selected for operations Q & R.
2nd.Day Tuesday 20th.Instr.W.S.Regt.	Q 10th.Bn."Queens"	W. to S.W.	Trenches 108-110 (300x front)100 smoke bombs,50 candles	6 pm.	6.4pm.	6.2 pm.	6.4 pm.	
3rd.Day Wednesday 21st.Inst.	R 21st.Bn.K.R.R.C.	do	Trenches 112-114 (280x front.100 smoke bombs 50 candles	5.30pm.	5.34 pm.	5.32 pm.	5.34 pm.	
4th.Day selected by Sector Commdr.	S 123rd.Inf.Bde	do	Trenches 101-102 (570x front)130 smoke bombs 65 candles	10 pm	10.4 pm	10.2 pm	10.4 pm.	Date selected not to coincide with operations P,Q or R

"C" Form (Original). Army Form C. 2123.

ED

MESSAGES AND SIGNALS. No. of Message ....

Prefix SM Code 5.20 Words 9	Received	Sent, or sent out	Office Stamp
£ s. d. Charges to collect	From ZH By Cpl Hell	At 5.21 p.m. To D26 By Cpl Hell	D26 20/6/16
Service Instructions. ZH			

Handed in at .... Office .... m. Received 5.21 m.

TO	D26

*Sender's Number	Day of Month	In reply to Number		AAA
BM486	20			
Barometer rising				

FROM: ZH

PLACE & TIME: 5.18 PM

* This line should be erased if not required.
Wt. 9771/4004. 75,000 Pads. 10/15. McC. & Co., Ltd., London. Forms/C.2123.

"A" Form. Army Form C. 2121.
MESSAGES AND SIGNALS No. of Message............

| Prefix S.M. Code FBP m. | Words 8 | Charge | This message is on a/c of : | Recd. at .... m. |
| Office of Origin and Service Instructions. D26 | Sent At 5.13 p.m. To 24 By Sgt Bury | | .... Service. (Signature of "Franking Officer.") | Date D26 From 24.... By |

TO { Z.4

| * Sender's Number AF 223 | Day of Month 20th | In reply to Number | AAA |

Big aaa

From D26
Place
Time 14.12 hrs

(Z) ACI Provence
Censor. Signature of Addressee or person authorised to telegraph in his name.

* This line should be erased if not required.

Appen J

On the night of the 20th June 1916 the Gas alarm was sounded by troops on our left ~~right~~ i.e. north of our position.

The gas cloud drifted down No mans land and was broken up by our artillery fire

The wind was light variable and the gas eventually appeared to be blown over the enemy lines

On the night of the 22nd June 1916 the gas alarm was sounded by troops on our right i.e South of our position.

No effect of gas was felt in any of our trenches

R O A Knight Lt Col

124th Bde
10 (S) Bn 41 July
R.W. Surrey Regt

Army Form C. 2118

WAR DIARY
INTELLIGENCE SUMMARY
(Erase heading not required.)

VOL 3

Place	Date	Hour	Summary of Events and Information	Remarks and references to Appendices
Trenches 103-112	1/7/16	—	Trenches - Wounded No 9/10259 Pte R ROBINSON AZ	
"	2/7/16	—	" - Heavy artillery fire by our Gunners - reply fairly well sustained. no casualties. AZ	
"	3rd	—	Trenches AZ.	
"	4th	—	Trenches. A Coy withdrawn from Lancashire Support trench to rest Billets at Croslow. AZ.	
"	5th	—	Went into rest billets at CRESLOW. Wounded No 7625 L.Cpl F.A. SMITH. AZ.	
Billets	6th	—	Rest billets AZ	
"	7th	—	" " AZ.	
"	8th	—	" " Wounded 9913 Pte E.C. FELL, slightly - at duty AZ	
"	9th	—	" " Wounded No 6463 L.C. H. ROBERTS AZ.	
"	10th	—	" " Wounded No trenches 112 to 120. 123rd Infantry Bde. on our right	
Trenches	11th	—	Took over trenches 112 to 120. 123rd Infantry Bde. on our right 26th Royal Fusrs on our left. AZ.	

WAR DIARY
or
INTELLIGENCE SUMMARY
(Erase heading not required.)

Army Form C. 2118

Place	Date	Hour	Summary of Events and Information	Remarks and references to Appendices
Jenchés	12th	—	Quiet – Wounded 6/9753 Pte G.F. ~~WHITE~~ WHITE – died of his wounds. AZ	
–"–	13th	—	Normal – Killed no 6643 Pte J. MILLER; Wounded no 10046 L.Cpl. H. EASTOP; 10401 Pte P. WRIGHT; 10373 Pte E. PERKINS. AZ	
–"–	14th	—	Normal – Wounded 21319 Pte F. HODSON; 6/9487 Pte J.G. WARREN; 10115 Pte A.G. BARBER. AZ	
–"–	15th	—	Normal. Killed no 9752 Pte C.J. DUMBLETON; Wounded 6/11236 Pte R.F. GOLDSACK; 6/10023 Pte C.A. ANDREWS. AZ	
–"–	16th	—	Normal – See appendices 1 & 2 for programme minor operations AZ 1 & 2 on dates 12.13.14 & 15th inst. AZ	
–"–	17th	—	Relieved in trenches by 21 K.R.R. Went into rest billet at Jeport. In the evening called for volunteers for special raiding party. 140 men required. Coveres have put their names thus - men. Officer selecty. Capt Sutherland Lt Hopkinson - 2nd Lt Burgess, 2nd Lt Ransom, 2nd Lt Selby –	

WAR DIARY
or
INTELLIGENCE SUMMARY

(Erase heading not required.)

Army Form C. 2118

Place	Date	Hour	Summary of Events and Information	Remarks and references to Appendices
Papot	18/7		In billets Papot. Raiding party left by another bus for the held near BAILLEUL.	
"	19/7		In billets PAPOT. Skeen in two hours 5-9 feet dive etc.	
"	20/7		In billets PAPOT.	
"	21st		" " "	
"	22nd		" " "	
Yrencho	23		Came into the trenches. Held the same line T112-120. A party of 150 new men under Capt. Dunkland as the officers were left in billets. They are training for a special duty. Wounded no 5/9468 Pte H. STOW; 5/6910 Pte E.D. ALLEN. H.	
"	24th		normal trenches H. Pte H. Stow died on the 24th	
Yrencho	25th		Yrencho no 5/9468 Pte H. Stow died on the 24th Wounded today 5/9908 Pte A. WHEADON. H.	

Place	Date	Hour	Summary of Events and Information	Remarks and references to Appendices
Trenches	26th	—	Trenches. Wounded G/10215 Pte. H.W. NEWBERRY, G/9590 Pte. F. GOUGH. Killed no 24993 Pte. E.F. COX, 25015 Pte. S. ROBINSON. M. Wounded Pte. G. NIGHTINGALE. DooB	
—	27	—	The following casualties occurred during a raid which was made on the enemy lines by a party of about 150 other ranks under Capt. G. Sutherland. Lieut. Stephenson & 2nd Lieut. Ranson. — Wounded Capt. F. SUTHERLAND, Lieut. J.A.L. HOPKINSON; 2nd LIEUT. W.F. SERBY; 2nd Lt. S.I. RANSON. Killed G/10134 Pte. J. DREW; G/6289 Pte. W.J. SPEAIGHT; G/11762 Pte. G. WAKELING; G/6747 Pte. S. BEADLE; G/6443 Pte. W.E. RAPSON; Died of Wounds G/10303 LCpl. W.C. HAYCOCK. Wounded G/9998 Pte. H.E. THOULLESS; G/9980 Pte. H. PARKER; G/2024 Pte. R. HUNT; L/1114 Pte. H. WALLS; G/2432 Pte. A.13. BRISTOW; G/9451 LCpl. J.L. BATH; G/2094 Pte. G. MARNEY; G/16344 Pte. H. POWELL; G/14655 Pte. G. HORTON; G/10033 Pte. F.T. SYKES; G/6833 Pte. T.H. MARTIN; G/11234 Pte. F.W. SEARLE; G/9995 Pte. T. HOYLLAR; G/10032	

Army Form C. 2118

WAR DIARY
or
INTELLIGENCE SUMMARY
(Erase heading not required.)

Place	Date	Hour	Summary of Events and Information	Remarks and references to Appendices
Trenches	24/4/16	—	Cpl. H. RATTLE; 6/9953 L.Cpl. E. MAYNARD; G/10155 Pte A. JONES; 6/9544 Sgt. A. MACKLIN; 6/12468 Pte W. MILLER; 6/9642 Sgt R.H. DIGGINS; 6/9960 Cpl T. COOPER; L/14049 Pte H. JONES; 6/9958 Pte O.R. MATTHEWS; 6/10029 Pte. C. WILLSHIRE; 6/12488| L.Cpl A. DAY; 6/10151 L.Cpl W.E. INGLE; 6/25441 Pte. A.R. ANDERSON; 6/11422 Pte W.W. PINCHES; 6/19482 Pte. F.G. BRADISH G/9455 Pte. G. FRANCIS; 6/10168 Pte R. KITCHLING; 6/10401 Pte. G.H. PARKER; 6/4218 Pte. J. HALL; 6/6948 Pte. J.C. HUNT; 6/10091 Pte T. J. BENFORD; 6/4504 Pte. & J.F. BARNES; 6/9429 L.Cpl JEFFRIES; 6/9481 Pte J. ASHLIN. Missing 2/9518 Sgt H. CLARKE; 6/10202 Pte D. ATKINS; 6/10222 Pte. T.R. HOUGHTON; 6/10212 Cpl. E.L. PARKIN; 6/9936 Pte. J. BARNES; 9/1741 Pte T. FINN 6/10327 Pte. G. HAVERTY. Wounded 2nd Lieut. H.D.G. ERECKSON; 6/10234 Pte. E.A. BLENNEY. Operation Orders attached. Sketch of trenches attached. Report on result of raid and copies of messages received attached.	appx 3 4 5
"		3 P.m.	The Batt. moved into the centre sector of the Division	

WAR DIARY
or
INTELLIGENCE SUMMARY

Army Form C. 2118

Place	Date	Hour	Summary of Events and Information	Remarks and references to Appendices
Yeneka	27th	3 P.m.	Holding TS 103-111 relieving the 10 R.W.Kent. Regt & 11th Bn The Queens. A.L.	
-"-	28"	—	normal - killed no 9/7719 Pte F. W. MILLINER. A.L.	
-"-	29"	—	normal. A.L.	
-"-	30	—	normal - killed no 9/7735 Pte E. FOSTER. Wounded Lt G.A.WEBB A.L.	
-"-	31	—	normal A.L.	

In the Field
31 /1/16

Wakely
Lieut Colonel
Commdg 10 Queens

Officer Commanding,
   10th.Bn."Queens" R.W.S.Regt.
   26th.Bn.Royal Fusiliers.
   32nd.Bn.Royal Fusiliers.
   21st.Bn.K.R.R.C.

Batteries will fire as follows:-

Night of 12/13th.	A/187	from	10pm.to 12 midnight.
	B/183	"	12pm.to 2 am.
	C/187	"	2am.to 4 am.
Night of 13/14th.	B/183	"	10pm.to 12 midnight.
	C/187	"	12pm.to 2 am.
	A/187	"	2am.to 4 am.
Night of 14/15th.	C/187th.		10pm.to 2 am.
	A/187	"	12 midnight to 2am.
	B/183	"	2am.to 4 am.

                                        Major,
                                Brigade Major,
12/7/16.   124th.Infantry Brigade.

SECRET.

124 I.B.
K547

Officer Commanding,
   10th.Bn."Queens" R.W.S.Regt.
   26th.Bn.R.Fusiliers.   187th.Bde.R.F.A.
   32nd.Bn.R.Fusiliers.   190th.Bde.R.F.A.
   21st.Bn.K.R.R.C.   228th.Fd.Co.R.E.
   124th.T.M.Btty.   237th.Fd.Co.R.E.
   124th.M.G.Coy.   171st.Tunnelling Co.R.E.

As retaliation may be expected after 1 am. 14/7/16 men should be kept under cover.

In such places at ST.YVES communication trench, trenches behind the CRUCIFIX, and LE GHEER and any other such places as the enemy are in the habit of shelling, should be avoided.

With reference to Brigade Order No.27 if weather conditions are favourable, the operation originally detailed to take place at 12.30 pm. on the 13th. will now take place at 12.30 pm. on the 14th.

O.C. Units in the line will ensure that all necessary preparations for the discharge of smoke have been made.

Units will be notified as to whether the operation will take place or not.

The code words mentioned in Operation order No.27 will be used.

E.B.North, Major,
Brigade Major,
124th.Infantry Brigade.

13/7/16.

SECRET. COPY No. 6.

124th. Infantry Brigade, Order No. 29.

The operations for July 12th, 13th, 14th. as detailed in 124th. Infantry Brigade Order No. 28 and amendment thereto, are cancelled.

Minor operations will be carried out in co-operation with the 41st. Divisional Artillery against the enemy trenches as follows:-

Night July 13th./14th, 10.30pm.
Dummy raid and artillery bombardment on hostile trenches at C 4 d 1.4½.

2am. Gas discharge from Trenches 124, 127, 128 and part of 129.

July 14th.
Smoke discharge by 124th. Infantry Brigade from front of trenches 112-124 accompanied by bombardment of enemy's front and support lines with shrapnel.

Night 14/15th.
Minor enterprise by 124th. Infantry Brigade against the hostile trenches N. of FACTORY FARM.
Working parties will be suspended after 1am. July 14th. and on night of July 14/15th.

The Zero Hour will be communicated to all concerned by Special D.R. on the evening of each Operation.

The result of each enterprise is to be reported "Priority" to Brigade Headquarters followed by detailed account in writing.

Please acknowledge.

E.B. North, Major,
Brigade Major
124th. Infantry Brigade.

13/7/16.

Issued at

	Copy No. 1	file
"	2	War Diary
"	3	41st. Divn.
"	4	122nd. Inf. Bde.
"	5	123rd. Inf. Bde.
"	6	10th. Bn. "Queens"
"	7	26th. Bn. R. Fusiliers.
"	8	32nd. Bn. R. Fusiliers.
"	9	21st. Bn. K.R.R.C.
"	10	124th. M.G. Coy.
"	11	124th. T.M. Btty.
"	12	187th. Bde. R.F.A.
"	13	190th. Bde. R.F.A.
"	14	228th. Fd. Co. R.E.
"	15	237th. Fd. Co. R.E.
"	16	171st. Tunnelling Co. R.E.

****

SECRET.   Copy No. 3
                    124th. Infantry Brigade Order No.35.

INTENTION. 1. In order to inflict considerable losses on the enemy, prevent him withdrawing troops from our front, capture prisoners, and do as much damage as possible, a combined raid by one company, 123rd. Infantry Brigade, and one company, 124th. Infantry Brigade, will be carried out on a date to be notified later, in accordance with the attached Time Table.

ARTILLERY 2. The above combined raid will be prepared and supported by the Divisional Artillery, supplemented by a group of Heavy Artillery.
Arrangements will be made for co-operation of Stokes Guns, *and Machine Guns*.

OBJECTIVES 3. (a) One company 123rd. Inf. Bde. will attack the hostile front and support line trenches in the RED HOUSE locality
(b) One company, 10th. Bn. "Queens" R.W.S. Regt. will attack the hostile front line trenches from U 28 a 3¼.8 to U 22 c 4.2 and the support trenches behind them.
Both the companies will be accompanied by demolition Companies, provided by the R.E.

ZERO HOUR 4. The time of Zero Hour will be notified to all concerned from Brigade Headquarters.

WATCHES. 5. Watches will be synchronised at 5 pm. on the day of attack.

REPORTZS 6. Result of the raid will be reported by PRIORITY telegram to Brigade Headquarters by the unit concerned followed by a detailed account in writing.

7. Please acknowledge.

                                         P. B. Roth Major,
                                              Brigade Major,
                                           124th. Infantry Brigade.

19/7/16.
Issued at   Copy No. 1   File
            "   2   War Diary
            "   3   10th. Bn. "Queens" R.W.S. Regt.
            "   4   26th. Bn. R. Fusiliers.
            "   5   32nd. Bn. R. Fusiliers.
            "   6   21st. Bn. K.R.R.C.
            "   7   124th. M.G. Coy.
            "   8   124th. T.M. Btty.
            "   9   187th. Bde. R.F.A.
            "   10   190th. Bde. R.F.A.
            "   11   228th. Fd. Co. R.E.
            "   12   237th. Fd. Co. R.E.
            "   13   42nd. A.T. Co. R.E.
            "   14   Spare.

TIME - TABLE OF OPERATIONS.

Date	Hour	Operations.
Y Day	All day	Wire cutting by Divl.Artillery & T.M's, and registration by Heavy Artillery.
Z Day	1 hour before Zero	Bombardment of points of attack by Heavy Artillery, Divl.Artillery, T.M's.& Stokes Guns in accordance with detailed programmes drawn up by C.R.A. & Inf.Bdes. Counter battery work by Heavy Artillery.
"	0.0 (Zero hour)	Bombardment lifts from hostile front line and barrages formed round localities to be attacked. Bombardment to continue on enemy support trenches. Attacking Companies advance from their positions of assembly against the hostile trenches.
"	0.10	Bombardment lifts from hostile support trenches. Barrages to continue until O.C.Enterprise in each sector notifies artillery that the party has returned to our trenches

*****

War Diary   Appendix 3

N.B.

With reference to para.6 of the attached scheme, the clearance of the S.1 line will not be undertaken until the front line has been cleared.

The left and centre C.T.Parties will, however, immediately work up and block their respective communication trenches.

=*=*=*=*=

O.C. 10th Queens

The Divnl Commander wrote all
success to the attack.

a.m.

26/7/16.   Major Genl.
                        Lawford   Bh Awley Lt Col
                        Divn 11th Divn   9.

War Diary

appen 5

OUR OPERATIONS.
(a) Raid.

At 12 midnight a company of the 10th.Bn."Queens", strength 4 Officers, 154 other ranks and 8 R.E., under Capt.Sutherland raided the enemy's trenches between U 22 c 4.2 and U 22 c 3.4.

At 12 midnight our artillery, which had bombarded the enemy's front line trench for an hour, lifted on to his S 2 line, and the raiding party advanced on the enemy's trench.

As soon as our bombardment lifted the enemy placed a heavy barrage on our front line trench and NO MAN'S LAND.

The raiding party sustained a number of casualties during the advance, including Capt.Sutherland, who was wounded.

On reaching the enemy's wire, which had been cut very thoroughly by our artillery, the raiding party encountered a party of Germans, probably 10 to 15 strong, outside the enemy trench. The raiders immediately bombed this party and charged them with the bayonet. Some of the enemy were killed outside their trench others escaped into it. The raiding party followed them up into the front line trench, which they found to have been almost knocked to pieces by our artillery.

They blocked the front line trench on both flanks and proceeded to clear it.

A large number of Germans were found dead in the front line trench. Many of these had been blown in pieces, and it is impossible to estimate the number of dead.

3 or 4 Germans who had probably escaped into the trench were bayonetted.

The raiding party found three dug-outs behind the parados which were intact. In these they secured several packs, helmets, and a number of papers.

3 communication trenches ran back from the front line to the S.1 line.

The right and left of these trenches had been blown in, but the centre one was passable.

Part of the raiding party made their way up this trench almost to its junction with the S 1 line.

At this point they were bombed by the enemy and a bombing fight ensued.

The enemy also fired machine guns from the S 1 line.

The fire from the M.G's went high.

The party were unable to penetrate the S 1 line.

During this time the right blocking party were attacked by enemy bombers coming along the front line trench.

The blocking party blocked the trench successfully and held the enemy until the order to withdraw was given.

The party remained in the enemy's trenches for 15 to 20 minutes.

In spite of the fact that 3 of the 4 Officers were wounded early on, and the remaining officer was wounded immediately after he ordered the withdrawal, practically all sections of the raiding party appeared to have followed out the instructions laid down for them.

During the withdrawal the enemy maintained a heavy artillery barrage and machine gun fire on NO MAN'S LAND and our front line trench.

Nearly all our casualties appear to have occurred during the advance and withdrawal across NO MAN'S LAND.

Identification obtained during the raid proved that the trench was held by the 104th.Regiment, SAXON, and a Machine Gun Coy. (normal)

Letters found in the dug-outs contained much useful information about ~~the~~ internal conditions in GERMANY.
 The wire had been completely cut by our artillery, except in the ditch which was easily crossed by ladders.
 Our artillery support throughout was most effective.
 Our casualties were ~~approximately:-~~
  4 Officers ~~kill~~ wounded.
  5 Other ranks killed.
 36 "   "   wounded.

4 missing including
Sgt Clarke - who is
believed to have been
killed in German
line -

Ro

Secret   Copy No 6

124th Infantry Brigade Order No 28.

12th July, 1916

1. Minor operations will be carried out by Infantry Brigades in co-operation with the 41st Divisional Artillery against the enemy's trenches as follows:—

   Night July 12/13th
   Simultaneous minor enterprise by 122 Infantry Brigade against trenches at M.15 a 7½ 6¼.

   Minor Enterprise by 123 Infantry Brigade against trenches at C 4 d 1 4½.

   2 am Gas discharge from trenches 124, 127, 128 and part of 129 as per 41st Divn. Order No 22 of July 8/16

   July 13th.
   12.30 p.m. Smoke discharge by 124th Infantry Brigade on front of trenches 112–124 accompanied by bombardment of enemy's front and support lines with shrapnel.

   Night July 13/14th
   Minor Enterprise of 124th Infantry Brigade against hostile trenches 17 of FACTORY FARM.

2. Working parties will be suspended on those nights between hours of 11 pm and 2 am. (3 am on night of 12/13th)

   The Zero hour will be communicated to all concerned by special D.R.
   Acknowledge.

                                                    Major
                                              Brigade Major
                                          124 Infantry Brigade

Copy No	1	File
"	2	War Diary
"	3	41st Division
"	4	122nd Inf. Bde.
"	5	123 do.
"	6	10 The Queens
"	7	26th Bn R. Fusrs
"	8	32 do
"	9	21 K.R.R.C.
"	10	124 M.G. Coy
"	11	124 T.M.B
"	12	187 Bde. R.F.A
"	13	190 do
"	14	228 Fd Coy R.E.
"	15	237 do
"	16	171 Tunnelling Co R.E.

SECRET.   Copy No. 1

124th Infantry Brigade Order No. 38.

With reference to 124th Infantry Brigade Order No.35 of the 19/7/16, the operations detailed therein will be carried out on the night of the 26/27th July.

On the night 26/27th July, smoke will be discharged from Trenches 120, 121-123 for three periods of two minutes each at intervals of 12 minutes.

The first discharge will commence at 1 hour before Zero.
                  will cease at 58 minutes "   "

The second discharge will commence at 46 mins. before Zero.
                  will cease at 44 minutes "   "

The third discharge will commence at 32 mins. before Zero.
                  will cease at 30 minutes "   "

This operation is intended to conceal flash of heavy trench mortars.

The time of Zero will be notified to all concerned by D.R.

Please acknowledge.

                                          E. B. North Major,
                                              Brigade Major,
24/7/16.   124th Infantry Brigade.

Issued at. 8.30 p.m.

Copy No. 1. File.
"   "   2. War Diary.
"   "   3. 41st Division.
"   "   4. C.R.A. 41st Division.
"   "   5. 122nd Infantry Brigade.
"   "   6. 123rd Infantry Brigade.
"   "   7. 10th Bn. "Queens" R.W.S.Regt.
"   "   8. 26th Bn. Royal Fusiliers.
"   "   9. 32nd Bn. Royal Fusiliers.
"   "   10. 21st Bn. King's Royal Rifle Corps.
"   "   11. 124th Machine Gun Company.
"   "   12. 124th Trench Mortar Battery.
"   "   13. 183rd. Brigade R.F.A.
"   "   14. 187th. Brigade R.F.A.
"   "   15. 228th Field Coy. R.E.
"   "   16. 237th Field Coy. R.E.

Secret   No 4

124th. Infantry Brigade.

Attack on Hostile Front and Support Lines
between U 22 c 4.2 and U 22 c 3.4., and
at U 28 a 3½.8½.

HEADQUARTERS
No. K 605
124th INFANTRY BRIGADE

(A). GENERAL IDEA.

A raiding party, strength 4 Officers, 154 other ranks, and 8 R.E., will raid the Hostile trenches between U 22 c 4.2 and U 22 c 3.4, and will kill or capture all enemy in the front line trench, will then work up the two main communication trenches and take the enemy's second support line between U 22 c 5½.3½ and U 22 c 5.4½.

A second raiding party, strength 1 Officer, 40 Other Ranks, and 4 R.E., will raid the enemy's front line trench at U 28 a 3½.8½, and will do as much damage as possible to machine gun emplacements and other defences between U 28 a 3½.8½ and U 28 a 4¾.9½.

(B). SPECIAL INSTRUCTIONS.

1. Hostile wire will be cut in front of and for 20 yards on either side beyond the points to be raided.

2. Four passages at intervals of 25 yards will be cut in our wire in front of trench 113 to enable the main raiding party to get out. These passages will be cut obliquely at an angle of 45° so as to conceal them from observation by the enemy. A similar passage will be cut in the wire in front of trench 112 to enable the second raiding party to get out.

3. Character of ground to be attacked.
   (a) Main Raid.
   About 25 yds. in front of the enemy's trench runs a ditch. This ditch is probably full of wire which it will be difficult for the artillery to destroy.
   35 or 40 yds. behind the front line trench is the support line S.1. From aeroplane photographs it appears probable that this line is not occupied. Three communication trenches run from the front line to the S.1 line, the centre of which is probably disused.
   70 or 80 yds. behind the S.1 line is the main support line S.2 approached by 2 communication trenches continuing through the S.1 line. Between the S.1 & S.2 lines about 50 yards behind the former runs a hedge and a ditch.
   There appear to be a number of dug-outs off the S.2 line. On the left flank of the part of the S.2 line to be attacked a long communication trench runs back to the reserve line.
   (b) Subsidiary Raid.
   In front of his original front line trench the enemy has constructed a second trench running parallel to the front line, the top of which has recently been covered. It is impossible to say whether this cover is a strong head cover or merely a screen to conceal the trench from aerial observation.

4. Artillery Co-operation.   & Stokes Guns
   At 1 hour before Zero Hour the artillery will open a heavy bombardment on the enemy's front line trenches. Under cover of this bombardment both raiding parties will cross the parapet, pass through our wire, and lie down in their formation of attack in the grass in front of our wire.
   At the Zero Hour the bombardment will lift on to the enemy's S.2 line, and a complete box barrage will be formed.
   At 10 minutes after Zero Hour, artillery barrage on portion of S.2 line to be attacked lifts to points in rear of S.2 line selected by G.O.C., R.A. Box barrage will continue till O.C. Enterprise notifies R.A. that operation is complete.

Main raiding party Composition & Distribution.

5. The Main Raiding party will be composed and distributed as follows:-
Group 1. 1 Officer, 10 N.C.O's & 70 men, subdivided as follows:-
Scouts, 1 N.C.O. and 4 men.
Right covering party 1 N.C.O. and 8 men.
Left Covering party 1 N.C.O. 8 men.
Left flanking party 1 N.C.O. 8 men.
Right blocking party 1 N.C.O. 8 men.
Left blocking party 1 N.C.O. 8 men.
Left C.T.party 1 Officer, 2 N.C.O's 13 men.
Centre C.T.party 2 N.C.O's 13 men.

Group 2 will consist of O.C. Raiding party, 2 other Officers 6 N.C.O's 46 men (Infantry), 2 N.C.O's 6 Sappers (R.E.) sub-divided as follows:-
Right party. 1 Officer, 2 N.C.O's 17 men (Infantry) 1 N.C.O. 3 Sappers (R.E.).
Centre Party. O.C. Raiding party, 2 N.C.O's 12 men.
Left Party. 1 Officer, 2 N.C.O's 17 men (Infantry) 1 N.C.O. 3 Sappers (R.E.).
Group 3. Bomb carrying party. 2 N.C.O's 20 men.

6. Detailed Composition of Main Raiding Party.
Group 1.Right and Left Blocking Parties:-
   1 N.C.O., 2 bayonet men, 2 throwers, 2 carriers 2 spare men.
   Centre C.T.Party:- 2 sections each as follows:-
   1 N.C.O., 2 bayonet men, 2 throwers, 2 carriers, 1 Scavenger with one of the two sections.
   Left C.T.Party:-   ditto.
Group 2.Right party:-   ditto.
Group 2.Left Party :-   ditto.

7. Method of conducting Raid.
At Zero Hour O.C. will give the signal to advance. Group 1, preceded by scouts, will advance in extended order on the enemy's front line trench, and will take up the following positions:-

Right covering party outside the enemy's trench at point "A" will cover the right flank of the raiding party.

Left covering party outside enemy's trench at point "G" will cover left flank of the Raiding Party.

Left flanking party will ½ way across NO MAN'S LAND cover left flank of RAIDING PARTY.

On reaching enemy's trench, scouts will join Group 2 centre party.

Right blocking party will enter enemy's trench at point "B" and will block the front line trench to the right, and the communication trench entering the front line at that point.

Left blocking party will enter the enemy's front line trench at point "F" and will block the front line trench to the left and the short trench running into the front line trench at that point.

Centre C.T. Party will enter the enemy's trench at point "C" and will bomb up the communication trench to the S.1 line at point "H". 1 N.C.O. and 5 men will be left at this point to block the continuation of the communication trench to the S.2 line and the continuation of S.1 to the right. The remainder of the party will turn left along S.1 bombing dug-outs and connecting with the left C.T. party.

Left C.T. party, 1 N.C.O. and 6 men will enter the enemy's trench at point "D" and will bomb up the communication trench to the S.1 line at "I". Should this communication trench be disused or impassable, this party will move left along the front line trench and work up the C.T. from point "E" following the other half of the left C.T. party. The Officer, and remaining N.C.O. and 6 men of left C.T. Party will enter the enemy's trench at point "E", and will move up left communication trench to point "I". At this point they will connect with the other half of their party. 1 N.C.O. and 5 men will be left at point "I" to block the continuation of the communication trench to the S.2 line and the continuation of the S.1 trench to the left. The Officer and remainder of the party will turn right along S.1 bombing any dug-outs and connecting with the centre C.T. Party.

The left and centre C.T. Parties will remain in the S.1 line until they receive orders from O.C. Raiding Party to attack S.2 line or to withdraw.

Group 2 will follow Group 1 in extended order at a distance of 20 yards, and will act as follows:-
Right party will enter and clear enemy's front line between points "C" and "B".

Left party will enter and clear enemy's front line between "C" and "F".

Centre party will enter enemy's front line at point "C".

O.C. Raiding party will retain direct control of centre party who will be employed in maintaining communication, and in carrying bombs forward to the blocking parties and advance sections of the raiding party.

Group 3 will be employed in carrying sacks of bombs from our front line trench to point "C", where a central bomb store will be formed. A tape will be taken out by the centre party to point "C" to guide group 3 in carrying bombs. The men of Group 3 who have brought bombs across will be employed in escorting prisoners, etc., and assisting wounded.

If the enemy are found to be holding the front line or front and S.1 lines in force, the raiding party will not proceed beyond the S.1 line. If these lines are not strongly held and are quickly cleared, O.C. Raiding party will order an attack upon the S.2 line.
This attack is not to be ordered until 10 minutes after the Zero Hour at which time the barrage on the S.2 line will lift to enemy positions in rear.
This attack will be made up the centre and left communication trenches by the centre and left C.T. Parties (less 2 groups each 1 N.C.O. and 5 men, left to block points "H" and "I") followed by right and left parties of Group 2.

4.

The Centre C.T. Party and right party of Group 2 will proceed up the centre communication trench, the Left C.T. Party and left party of group 2 proceeding up the left communication trench.

On reaching S.2 trench at "K" 1 N.C.O. and 6 men of the right party will turn right for 30 yards and will block trench S.2 at about "K". The remainder of the party will turn left along S.2, clear the S.2 line, bomb dug-outs and connect with the party coming up the left communication trench.

The party coming up the left communication trench will enter the S.2 line at point "L". 1 N.C.O. and 4 men will block the communication trench at point "M". 1 N.C.O. and 4 men will block S.2 at point "N". The remainder of the party will turn right along trench S.2, will clear the trench, bomb dug-outs and connect with the party on their right.

R.E. will lay charges in the S.2 line so as to do as much damage as possible. On the order to withdraw from the S.2 line being given, the fuses of these charges will be lit. These fuses must be of sufficient length to enable the raiding party to withdraw safely. If the S.2 line is not reached, R.E. will use their charges to the best effect in the front line or S.1 line.

On trench S.2 being cleared of the enemy the Senior present Officer will order the party to ~~withdraw~~ reform. This order must not be given later than Zero 35 mins., and will be given earlier if the trench has been cleared.

The raiding parties will withdraw down the same communication trenches up which they have advanced, the blocking parties at "K.1", "N", and "M" withdrawing last in that order. The blocking parties left at "H" and "I" will follow the S.2 raiding party in their withdrawal.

At 00.40, O.C. Raiding Party in front line trench will blow two long, followed by two short, blasts on his whistle, and will send up 3 'Very' lights simultaneously as a signal to withdraw. On this signal the whole of the raiding party will withdraw, the blocking parties at "B" and "F", and covering parties at "A" and "G" and left flank party at "L" withdrawing last, and forming a rearguard to the raiding party.

8. Subsidiary Raiding Party. Composition and Distribution.

The raiding party on U 28 a 3½.8½ will consist of :-
1 Officer, 6 N.C.O's and 34 men (Infantry) 1 N.C.O. 3 sappers R.E.
Distribution:- Scouts, 1 N.C.O. 2 men.
Right group, 2 N.C.O's 12 men.
Left group 2 N.C.O's 14 men (Infantry)
1 N.C.O. 3 Sappers (R.E.)
Bomb carrying party. 1 N.C.O. 6 men.
Detailed Composition.
Right Group:- 2 Sections, each of 1 N.C.O., 2 bayonet men, 2 throwers, 2 carriers.
Left group :- 2 sections, each of 1 N.C.O., 2 bayonet men, 2 throwers, 2 carriers, 1 spare man.

9. Method of conducting raid.

At Zero Hour O.C. Party will give the signal to advance.
The party will advance in extended order in one line, preceded by scouts, the right group on the right, the left group on the left. Great care must be taken by the party to enter the enemy's trench at point "O". The wire will be cut for 20 yds. on each side of this point, but will not have been cut further to the left.

On reaching the enemy's trench, the right group will turn to the right, 1 N.C.O. and 6 men going down the outer trench and 1 N.C.O. and 6 men going down the inner trench. They will clear this trench as far as points "P" and "P.1" and will block it from that point until the left group withdraw. Left Group; on reaching the enemy's trench, 1 N.C.O. and 7 men will turn left, down the outer front line trench, 1 N.C.O. and 7 men will turn left down the inner trench. They will clear these trenches as far as points "Q" and "Q.1" and will block the front line trenches at these points. They will be followed down the inner trench by the R.E. party who will lay charges under machine gun emplacements or other works disposing of their charges so as to do as much damage as possible to the trench. If the outer trench is found to have been entirely demolished by our bombardment the sections of the raiding party detailed to deal with the outer trench will follow the inner trench party in the inner trench. O.C. raiding party will remain near the point of entry with the scouts, and will keep in touch with both groups of his raiding party.

The bomb carrying party will be employed in carrying sacks of bombs across to the enemy's trench at "O" (to which point a tape will be taken by the raiding party) and assisting the wounded to return.

The party will remain in the trench for 35 minutes if possible. After 35 minutes O.C. Raiding party will sound three blasts on his whistle. On this signal the R.E. will light their charges which should have a fuse of sufficient length to enable all the party to withdraw and the party will withdraw.

9. **Scavengers.**
Each section of the raiding parties employed in clearing trenches will detail one man to collect German S.A.A., shoulder straps, papers, etc. This man will carry a sandbag and a sharp knife. He must be instructed that all German Soldiers carry a Pay Book and often a note book in their tail coat pockets.

10. A telephone and 1 N.C.O. and 4 Signallers will accompany O.C. Raiding party.
Tapes will be taken out by the right and left covering parties to "A" & "G" to guide the party in their withdrawal. 1 N.C.O. and 8 stretcher bearers will be with the centre group under O.C. Raiding party

11. Heavy Rifle, Lewis and Machine Gun Fire will be maintained throughout the raid upon the flanks of the raiding parties, care being taken that such fire is directed well to the left flank of covering and flank parties on left. Vickers and Lewis Gunners will use stakes to prevent their guns traversing beyond the flanks.

12. **Arms and Equipment, etc.**
(a) All ranks will wear a white brassard on the right arm.
(b) Officers will carry revolvers, and knob-kerries.
(c) Scouts:- Rifles, bayonets, bomb waistcoats.
(d) Covering parties:- Rifles, bayonets, bomb waistcoats, bandolier of ammunition. 1 sack of bombs per party.
(e) Left flanking party:- Rifles, bayonets, bomb waistcoats bandolier of ammunition.
(f) N.C.O's:- Rifles, or knobkerries, bayonets, bomb waistcoats.

(g) Bayonet men:- Rifles, bayonets, bomb waistcoats.
(h) Throwers:- Knobkerries and bomb waistcoats.
(i) Carriers:- Slung rifles, bomb waistcoats, sack of 15 bombs.
(j) Spare men:- Rifles bayonets, bomb waistcoats.
(k) Bomb carrying parties:- Slung rifles, bayonets, sack of 15 bombs.
(l) Scavengers:- Bomb waistcoats, knob-kerries, sharp knives.

Blocking parties will carry intrenching tools and 2 sandbags in the belt. Blocking parties at 'B', "F", "Q" "Q.1" will carry two picks per party. Blockers at "H", "I", "K.1", "M", "N", "P", "P.1", one pick per party.
All other ranks armed with rifles and not detailed to carry a bandolier, will carry 30 rounds S.A.A. ~~in their~~

One man at least in each party entering the hostile trenches will carry wire-cutters and an electric torch.
All wires in enemy's trenches will be cut.
Main party will carry 8 short ladders for crossing ditch in enemy's wire.

13. **Medical arrangements.**
Wounded will be brought to Railhead S.119 via Gap "G" C.T.116, S.118. Trolleys will be stationed at Railhead for the conveyance of wounded.

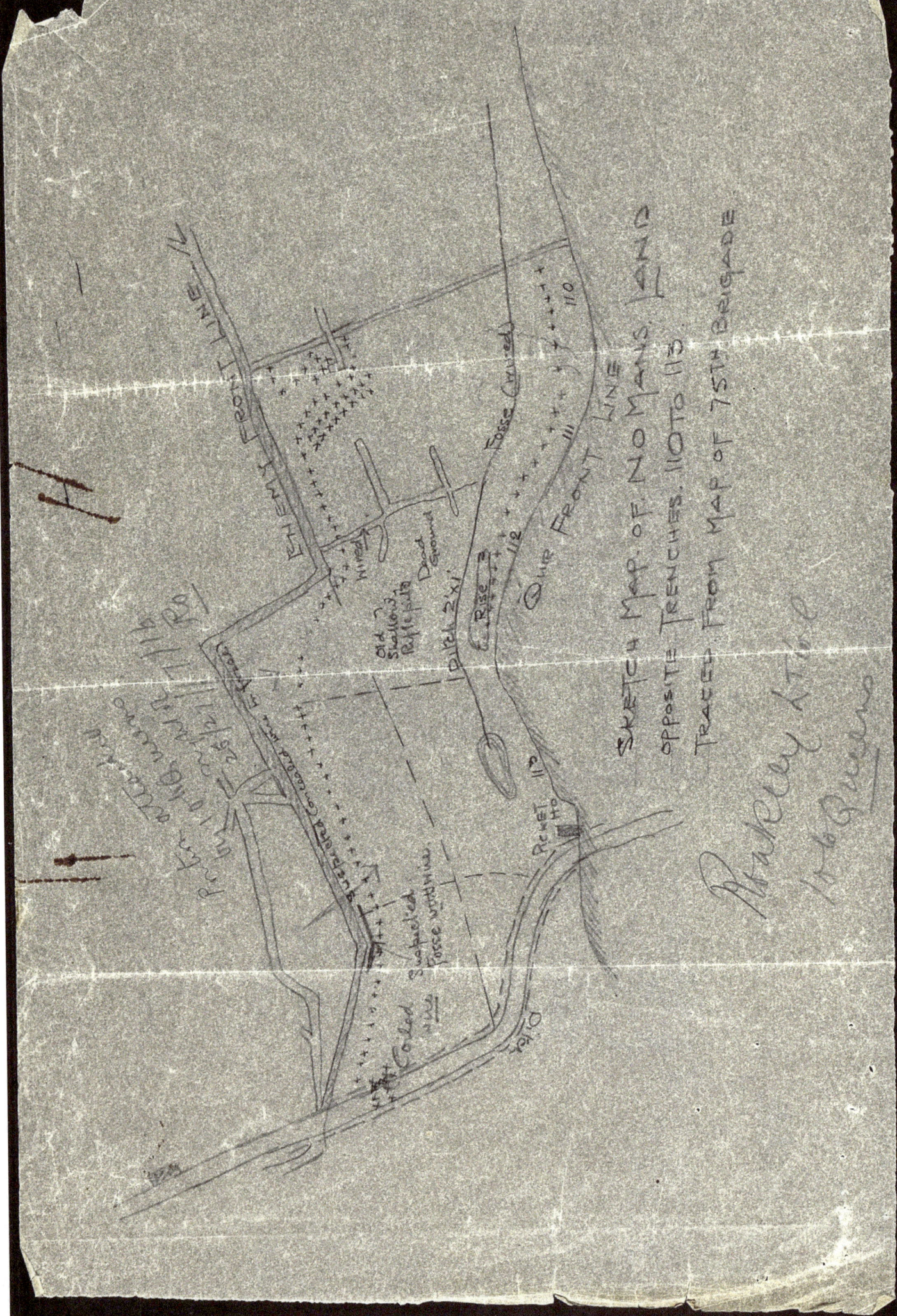

Messages in connection with Raid 26th/27th July '16

I. **Army Commander.** The Army Commander wishes his congratulations conveyed to all concerned on the successful raid carried out last night which inflicted much loss on the enemy

II. **G.O.C. 41st Div.** "Please convey to all ranks of the party of the 10th Bn. "Queens" who took part in the raid on the German trenches last night, my congratulations on the gallant manner in which they carried out the enterprise."

III. **G.O.C. 124 Inf Bde.** The G.O.C 124th Infantry Brigade desires to associate himself with the congratulations of the G.O.C. 41st Division, and to say how much he, and the whole of the Brigade appreciate the manner in which the enterprise was carried out by all ranks.

RO
Lt Col
10th Queens.

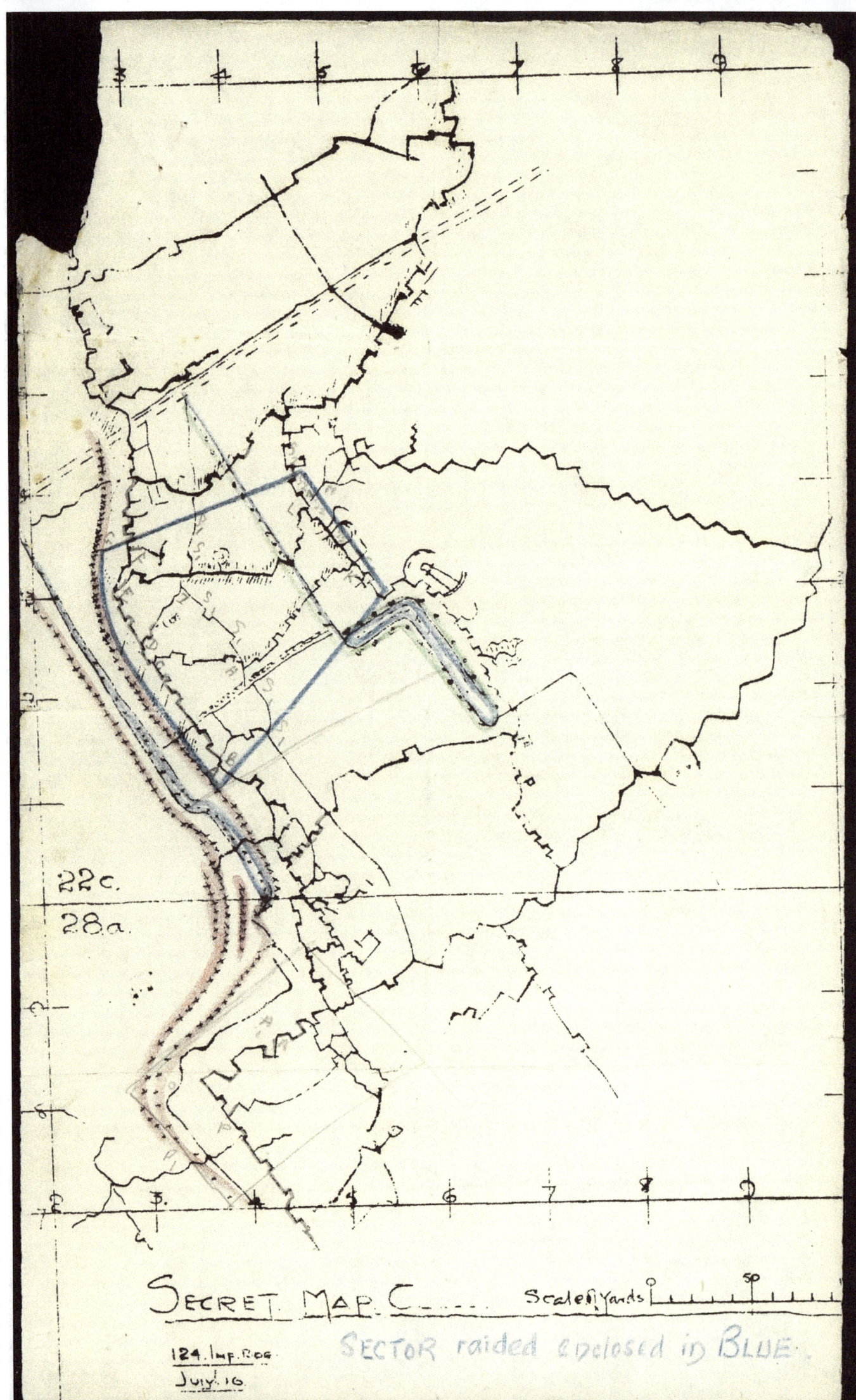

WAR DIARY
INTELLIGENCE SUMMARY

Army Form **VO4**

August, 1916

10 Queens

Place	Date	Hour	Summary of Events and Information	Remarks and references to Appendices
Trenches	1/8/16	—	Battn. occupied Trenches 103 – 111 being the right Bn of the centre sector of the 41st Division. The trenches on our right are held by the 123rd I.Bde. During the day the following casualties occurred :— Wounded no 6/10301 L/Sgt G. GOODMAN. Killed no 6/10058 Sergt. A.H. CHEESEMAN. A.F.	
"	2/8/16	—	Operations in this sector normal. The following previously reported missing are now believed to have been killed:— no 6/10222 Pte R. HOUGHTON. 6/9766 Pte H.A. ATKINS. J.B.	
Soyer Farm	3"	—	We were relieved in the trenches by the 12 Bn East Surrey Regiment and moved to Rest Billets. A Coy at GRANDE RABEQUE, B Coy at SOYER FARM, C Coy at DELENNELLE, D Coy at TILLEUR. Head Quarters at SOYER FARM. The following casualties were caused by shell fire at GRANDE RABEQUE :— Killed 6/9956 Pte. W. DENTON; No 6/9956 Pte. W.H. MOORE; Wounded {No 6/10139 Pte W. DENTON; No 6/9771 Pte F.F. SHADDICK. J.F.B.	

Army Form C. 2118

WAR DIARY
or
INTELLIGENCE SUMMARY
(Erase heading not required.)

Instructions regarding War Diaries and Intelligence Summaries are contained in F. S. Regs., Part II. and the Staff Manual respectively. Title Pages will be prepared in manuscript.

Place	Date	Hour	Summary of Events and Information	Remarks and references to Appendices
Red Bdds.	4/8/16	—	Normal.— Battn. employed on fatigues. JnoB.	
"	5/8/16	—	Normal.— Battn. employed on fatigues. JnoB.	
"	6/8/16	—	Normal.— 2nd Anniversary of outbreak of war commemorated — no fatigues. JnoB	
"	7/8/16	—	Normal.— Battn. employed on fatigues — our artillery active all day. JnoB.	
"	8/8/16	—	Normal.— Quiet. Casualties:— Wounded No 21/9751 Pte. A. TOWNSEND. JnoB	
		5.30 p.m.	One Company relieved a Coy. of 12 East Surreys in the trenches. JnoB	
"	9/8/16	5 A.M.	Remaining 3 Coys. of the Battn. relieved remaining 3 Coys. of 12th East Surreys in the trenches. A Coy. right firing line (T.109-111.) D Coy. in reserve FUSILIER TERRACES. B Coy. left firing line (T103-108.) Normal. Entry 8/5/16. No 21/9751 Pte. A. TOWNSEND — Not wounded. JnoB.	
"	10/8/16	—	Normal.— Entry very quiet. JnoB.	

Army Form C. 2118

WAR DIARY
or
INTELLIGENCE SUMMARY
(Erase heading not required.)

Instructions regarding War Diaries and Intelligence Summaries are contained in F. S. Regs., Part II. and the Staff Manual respectively. Title Pages will be prepared in manuscript.

Place	Date	Hour	Summary of Events and Information	Remarks and references to Appendices
Trenches	11	—	Normal H.	
"	12	—	Normal — Killed 9/11759 Pt. F. ALEXANDER. H.	
"	13	—	Normal H.	
"	14	—	Normal — Enemy Artillery a little more active H.	
"	15	—	Normal. H.	
"	16	—	Normal. H.	
Souttu-Farm.	17	—	Normal. We were relieved in the trenches by the 9th Bn. Yorks. & Lancs. Regt. H.	
NOOTE BOOM	18	—	Normal — The Battn. was relieved in Rat-Burets by the 8th Yorks. Regt. and marched to billets at NOOTE BOOM Area H.	
"	19	—	Quiet. H.	
"	20	—	Quiet — route marching drill etc. H.	
"	21	—	" Inspected by G.O.C. Bde. H.	
"	22	—	" Route march and drill etc. Job	
"	23	—	" The Battn. moved to BUIGNY L'ABBÉ. Entrained at NOOTE BOOM at 6.30 PM Detrained PONT REMY 2.30 p.m. – Marched to BUIGNY L'ABBÉ. Job	

Army Form C. 2118

WAR DIARY
or
INTELLIGENCE SUMMARY
(Erase heading not required.)

Instructions regarding War Diaries and Intelligence Summaries are contained in F. S. Regs., Part II. and the Staff Manual respectively. Title Pages will be prepared in manuscript.

Place	Date	Hour	Summary of Events and Information	Remarks and references to Appendices
BUIGNY L'ABBÉ	24/8/16	—	Billets – Baths, training & drill. Jno.B.	
"	25/8/16	—	" Company in attack – mostly Drill. Jno.B.	
"	26/8	—	" Coy training in semi open tactics. H.	
"	27/8	—	" Sunday. Inspections, Bathing etc. H.	
"	28	—	" Training H.	
"	29	—	" " H.	
"	30	—	" Training H.	
"	31	—	" Training H.	
			Nothing unusual has taken place during our tour in billets. H.	

31/8/16

Morley
Lieut. Colonel
Commanding. 10 Queens.

Army Form C. 2118

WAR DIARY
or
INTELLIGENCE SUMMARY
(Erase heading not required.)

10th Bn. THE QUEENS R.W. SURREY REGT.

SEPTEMBER 1st/14th

Place	Date	Hour	Summary of Events and Information	Remarks and references to Appendices
BUIGNY l'ABBE	1/9/16	—	Training - Bn in attack form'n.	
—"—	2/9/16	—	Training - Bn in attack - wood fighting - night march form'n.	
—"—	3/9/16	—	Bathing - Distribution of decorations to Sgt KING, Pte PHILLIPPE & Pte CRICHTON by G.O.C. 41st Div'n. Bn. Church Parade. form'n.	
—"—	4/9/16	—	Training. Inspection of Bn by GOC 41st Div. form'n.	
—"—	5/9/16	,	Training form'n.	
—"—	6/9/16	,	Training form'n.	
—"—	7/9/16	—	Bn marched to LONGPRÉ - entrained at LONGPRÉ - detrained RIBEMONT - marched to DERNANCOURT AREA & bivouced there. form'n.	
Camp	8/9/16	—	Training form'n.	
—"—	9/9/16	—	Bn marched from DERNANCOURT AREA to point ½ mile N. of MEAULTE & bivouaced there. form'n.	
—"—	10/9/16	—	Training form'n.	
—"—	11/9/16	—	Training form'n.	
—"—	12/9/16	—	Training form'n.	
—"—	13/9/16	—	Bn moved from bivouac ½ mile N of MEAULTE towards POMMIERES REDOUBT. Bn reached POMMIERES REDOUBT at 2-30 A.M. - Conducted by guides of the 10th R.W. Kent Regt to trenches on N.E. side of DELVILLE WOOD.	
—"—	14/9/16	—		

Army Form C. 2118

WAR DIARY
10th Bn "The Queen's" R.W. Surrey Regt.
INTELLIGENCE SUMMARY SEPTEMBER

(Erase heading not required.)

Instructions regarding War Diaries and Intelligence Summaries are contained in F.S. Regs., Part II. and the Staff Manual respectively. Title Pages will be prepared in manuscript.

Place	Date	Hour	Summary of Events and Information	Remarks and references to Appendices
Trenches	14/9/16	—	Distribution - A Coy right front line, B Coy left front line, C Coy left front reserve, D Co right reserve - Relief completed 10am. - orders for attack	
"	15/9/16	—	on 15/9/16 issued to Coys 5 p.m. JnoB. Bn assaulted enemy trenches - 4 lines - in immediate front - took FLERS & occupied enemy trenches immediately N.E. of FLERS. JnoB.	
"	16/9/16	—	Bn twice counter attacked but repulsed enemy. JnoB.	
"	17/9/16	—	Bn moved back into Support in GREEN & BROWN TRENCH on right of FLERS ROAD. JnoB.	
"	18/9/16	—	Normal. JnoB.	
"	19/9/16	—	Bn. was relieved & moved into DERNANCOURT Area. JnoB.	
Buire	20/9/16	—	Training. JnoB.	
"	21/9/16	—	" JnoB.	
"	22/9/16	—	" JnoB.	
"	23/9/16	—	" JnoB.	
"	24/9/16	—	" JnoB.	
"	25/9/16	—	" JnoB.	
"	26/9/16	—	" JnoB.	
"	27/9/16	—	" JnoB.	
"	28/9/16	—	" JnoB.	
"	29/9/16	—	" JnoB.	
"	30/9/16	—	" JnoB. I certify that whilst the battalion is in front state inf eff	

Talbot Jarvis
Major
Comdg 10th Bn The Queens Rgt

NOMINAL ROLL OF OFFICERS, N.C.O's AND MEN - KILLED, WOUNDED AND MISSING ON 15th, 16th, AND 17th SEPT. 1916.

Lt.Col.R.Oakley - Wounded.
Capt. & Adjt.A.Lawrence - Wounded 15th
                 - died of wounds 19/9/16.
Capt. D.C.Johnston - Wounded.
Capt. F.Hayley Bell - Wounded.
Capt. M.Bessell - Killed.
Capt. J.B.Dodge - Wounded.
Capt. A.F.Robson - Wounded.
2/Lt.A.F.Berrange - Wounded.
  " F.J.Heath - Wounded.
  " H.E.Mance - Killed.
  " F.Baker - Died of wounds 18/9/16
  " E.Savereux - Wounded
  " R.C.Javes - Killed
  " R.W.Scott - Wounded
  " E.Cox - Wounded
  " R.A.Hawes - Wounded
  " J.S.Cashel - Wounded
Lt.T.W.Sweetnam R.A.M.C.attd. 10th "Queen's" wounded.

"A" COMPANY

G/10117 Pte Allen A. - Missing
G/10080 L/Cpl.Brading C. - Wounded
G/9936 Pte Barnes J. - Wounded
G/9945 L/Cpl.Bailey G.H. - Wounded
G/9372 Pte Barwick P. - Wounded
10118 Pte Baldwin A. - Wounded
G/9769 Pte Beagley G. - Wounded
G/11767 " Browning R. - Wounded
G/7633 " Bugden G. - Wounded
G/7777 Cpl.Bryant M. - Wounded
G/10122 Pte Britt F.G. - Wounded
G/10124 " Burnham R. - Wounded
G/25990 " Bacon S.J. - Wounded
G/10125 " Bull W.R. - Wounded
G/14623 " Britnell F. S.Wd.at duty.
G/5777 Cpl.Clowser G. - Wounded.
G/10132 L/Cpl.Cox W.T. - Wounded
G/5978 Pte Childs J.H. - Wounded.
G/9937 Pte Claridge H. - Wounded.
G/25204 " Clifford H. - Wounded
G/25217 Pte Catlin A. - Wounded.
G/9693 " Curtis A.L. - Wounded.

G/7373 Cpl.Crease F.G. - Wounded.
G/10000 Pte Cooper J. - Missing.
G/10022 Sgt.Dibble H.W. - Wounded.
G/7544 L/Cpl.Draper J. - Wounded.
G/10051 Cpl.Dann H. - Missing. Wounded
G/10069 Pte Davis T. - Missing.
G/7616 " Dawes S.C. - Missing.
G/10139 " Denton W. - Missing.
G/10071 " Day T.H. - Wounded.
G/24979 " Dickson T.D. - Wounded.
G/24762 " Entwhistle W. - Missing.
G/9950 " Edwards G.H. - Missing.
G/24984 " Evans R. - Wounded.
G/9383 " Esling G. - Wounded.
G/10068 " Fountain - Killed.
G/24876 " Finch F. - Missing.
G/7711 " Finn F. - Missing.
G/7260 " Ford W. - S.Wd.at duty.
G/10145 " Clithero T. - Killed.
G/10252 Sgt.Green T.C. - Wounded.
G/6568 L/Sgt.Goldsmith E. - Wounded.
G/7545 Cpl.Harris A. - Wounded.

(Continued)

G/9790 Pte Haysom AR. -S.Wd.at duty.
G/7736 " Humphreys N.-Wounded.
G/24995 " Hills R. -Wounded.
G/9429 " Hibbard C.J.-Shell shock.
G/9986 " Hammatt P. -Wounded.
G/7131 " Hill H.A. -Wounded.
G/10150 " Hughes C. -Wounded.
G/10147 " Hinds L.G. -Wounded.
G/9443 " Hampton D. -Wounded.
G/5919 " Jennings W. -Wounded.
G/10155 " Jones A.E.-Wounded.
G/7654 " Jones A.R.-Missing. *Wounded*
G/24877 " James SJ -Missing.
G/9982 " Jefferis F.A.-Wounded.
×G/11213 " Jephson A. Jones W.-Wounded. *Wounded*
G/24765 " Jones R. -Wounded.
G/9448 " Sgt.King F.J.-Wounded.
G/6554 " Love C. -Wounded.
G/6839 " Sgt.Mayhead W. -Wounded.
G/10161 " Miles S. -Missing.
G/9992 " Markwell HP.-Wounded.
G/9622 Sgt.Newton J.-Wounded.
G/9984 Pte.Parry D.J.-Wounded.
G/6980 " Powell T.V.-Wounded.
G/10432 " Roberts F.-Missing.
G/9996 " Roberts FF.-Wounded
G/10183 L/Cpl.Stanton J.-Wounded.
G/9957 Pte Smith F.-Missing.
G/9414 " Smith P.-Missing. *Wounded*
G/10173 " Smithdale E.A.-Missing.
G/10083 " Salt E.-Wounded.
G/11775 " Self F.-Wounded.
G/9969 " Shean M.-Wounded.
L/11270 " Spencer J.-Wounded.
G/11772 " Turner R.-Wounded.
G/7737 " Tutt S.-Wounded.
G/9773 " Toms H. S.Wd. at duty.
G/9494 " Welling F.-Wounded.
G/9483 " Wells A.-Wounded.
S/7001 " Webb J. S.Wd. at duty.
G/9463 " White W.H.-Wounded.
G/9499 " Winspear J.-Wounded.
G/7543 " Wells H.-Missing. *Wounded*
G/7572 " Wilkinson F.-Missing.
G/9455 L/Cpl.Walker N.-Killed.

"B" COMPANY

G/9568 Sgt.Andrews HC.-Wounded.
G/9966 Pte Amos W.H.-Wounded.
G/10001 " Ayres H.J.-Wounded.
G/10238 " Allder P.W.-Wounded.
G/10240 " Archer C.H.-Wounded.
G/9520 " Barrington C.-Killed.
G/9782 Pte Bradish F.G.-Wounded.
G/10228 " Barber A. S.Wd. at duty
G/10193 " Brown W.F.-Wounded.
G/10186 " Barratt W.-Wounded.
G/10203 " Burnage AF.-Wounded.
G/10204 " Bustin C.-Wounded.
G/11773 " Bond TH.-Wounded.
G/7272 " Pte Britcher AR-Wounded
G/7644 " Brown W.-Killed.
G/9555 " Crichton A.-Wounded
G/9922 " Cook A.-Wounded.
G/10248 " Cleaver M.-Wounded
G/7716 " Collins WC-Wounded.
G/7715 " Cook A.-Killed.
G/4955 " Cook H.-Wounded.
G/12600 L/Sgt.Chapman HL-Wounded
G/10131 Cpl.Cook H.-Wounded.
G/10867 Pte Dunn W.-Missing.
G/9672 Sgt.Diggins RH.-Wounded
G/9609 Pte Galvin CH -S.Wd. at duty.
L/11265 L/Cpl.Hickman WF -Wounded.
G/9506 Pte Humphreys J.-Wounded
G/7732 " Hall BW.-Wounded.
G/7647 " Hageman A.-Wounded.
G/11786 " Hopkins F.-Wounded.
G/9418 " Hawksworth T.-Missing *Wounded*
G/9436 " Idle A.-Died of wounds.
G/9583 " L/Cpl.Ireson F. S.Wd. at duty.
G/9790 " Jones S.B.-Wounded.
G/10221 " Johnson FG.-Wounded.
G/9791 L/Cpl.Jones WF-Wounded.
G/6523 L/Sgt.Kitts J.-Wounded
G/6566 L/Cpl.Knott.W.-Wdd.
G/9569 Pte.Kinchin.W.T.-Wdd.
G/7341 " Kiddle.A.F. " "
G/10218 " Letts.S. " "

(Continued)

G/10438 Pte. Lucas.A. – Wounded.
G/14676 " Lemar.S. "
G/24997 " Lucas.L. S.Wd. at duty.
G/10028 Sgt. Mitchell.A. Wounded.
G/10016 Pte. Mildenhall.A. Died of Wds.
G/7419 " Morgan.A.J. – Wounded.
G/11784 " Mitchell.A.M. – "
G/10211 L/Cpl.Noakes.W.G. "
G/9754 Cpl. Page.H. "
G/7636 L/Cpl.Rigdan.H.A. "
G/9789 Pte. Russell.F.F. "
G/11785 " Russell.W.C. – Missing.
G/24144 " Redman.S. – Wounded.
G/25106 " Smith.R.V. "
G/25000 L/Cpl.Scott.A. "
G/9514 Pte. Sexton.H. "
G/10010 " Sartain.F. Missing.
G/6771 " Sampson.A. Wounded.
G/10417 " Shinn.W. "

G/7727 Pte Smisson J.W. – Wounded.
G/7778 Pte Symonds R. – Wounded & Missing.
G/6333 " Standing G. – Wounded & Missing.
G/868 " Sevenoaks A. – Killed.
G/10009 Cpl.Trunchion A. – Wounded.
G/10225 L/Cpl.Waite G. – Killed
G/12462 " Walker W.H. – Wounded.
G/7443 " Warner W. – Killed.
G/25018 Pte Virden A. – Wounded.
G/7638 Pte West.R.A. Wounded.
G/11768 Pte Warren J. – Wounded.
G/10194 Pte York F.G. – Wounded/Missing.
G/10207 Pte Evans T.H. Wounded.
G/10244 " Eyles J.R. – Wounded.
G/10263 " Eaton W.L. – Wounded.
G/10098 " Eldridge F.F. – Wounded
G/9528 " Fulkes WG – Wounded
G/9795 " Faulkner A. – Missing.
G/10214 " Fairhead A. – Wounded.
G/10223 " Farnsworth F. – Missing.
G/7700 " Field P. – Killed
G/25787 " Facer W. – Wounded
G/9557 " Green A. – Wounded
G/10092 " Grimshaw A. – Wounded
G/10232 " Gallant P. – Missing

G/25226 Pte Sargent F. – Missing.
G/24518 " Smith F.C. – Missing.
G/9563 " Theobald A. – Wounded.
G/9588 " Torode J.G. – Wounded
G/9591 " Torode W.H. – Killed
G/24160 " Thorn W. – Killed

"C" COMPANY

G/9356 L/Cpl.Burford G. – Wounded.
G/10306 Pte Bird BF – Killed
G/7526 " Purberry A. – Killed.
G/9796 " Bean H. – Wounded
G/10280 " Butler S. – Wounded.
G/9708 " Baynes GH – Missing.
G/9727 " Bright T. – Wounded
G/9519 Sgt.Campbell J. – S.Wd. at duty
G/9599 L/Sgt.Combes HW. – Wounded
G/9542 Cpl. Crouter FA – Wounded
G/11753 L/Cpl.Crabb A. – Killed.
G/10429 " Chapman F. – Wounded
G/6790 Pte Carpenter J. – Killed.
G/9705 " Dunn C.J. – Wounded
G/6642 " Edser R.H. – Wounded.
G/6748 " Edwards W. – Wounded
G/10437 " Faulkner F. – Wounded.
G/11779 " Freeman W. – Wounded.
G/9750 " Fuller RA – Wounded.
G/9978 " Godfrey C. – Died of Wounds
G/10261 L/Cpl.Hewlett JW – Wounded.
G/10030 Pte Harwood T. – Missing.
G/10298 " Johnson W. – Wounded.
G/9979 L/Cpl.Kreuter W. – Wounded
G/9664 Pte Lewis FW – Missing.
G/12456 " Lightfoot J. – Wounded
G/10260 " Lamb WC. – Wounded.
G/9683 " Lake CJ. – Wounded.
G/9712 L/Cpl.Morgan T. – Wounded.
G/9711 Pte Meatyard AR – Wounded
G/7515 " Prince W. – Wounded.
G/7745 Cpl.Reynolds SC – Wounded.
G/14336 Pte Pice J. – Wounded.
G/25811 " Radbourne W. – Missing.
G/2844 " Rostrom R. – Missing.
G/9665 " Regan H. – Wounded.
G/7646 " Sheaffe W. – Wounded
G/9772 " Smith CR – Missing
9739 – Dadswell WC Wounded
10299 – Maycock S " at duty
10259 – Dawn W "

G/9635 Pte Shenstone F. - Wounded
G/9756 " Steggall F. - Wounded
G/10335 " Skelham P. - Wounded
G/10313 " Scott HV.S.Wd. at duty.
G/9668 Sgt.Taylor GH - Wounded.
G/11272 Pte Thacker F. - Missing.
G/11234 Pte Trow P. - Wounded
G/2287 " Turner G. - Wounded
G/10292 L/Cpl.Wallace C. - Wounded.
G/10309 Pte. Whiteman C. - Wounded
G/10337 Pte Wootton WH. - Missing.

"D" COMPANY

G/7623 Pte Andrews JH - Wounded
G/9423 Sgt.Butler C. - Wounded
G/9836 Pte Bastin TH. - Wounded
G/10348 Pte Bradford DH - Wounded
G/10384 Pte Blackwell A. - Wounded
G/6450 Sgt.Brindley H. - Killed
G/6736 Pte Baker T. - Wounded
G/10231 Cpl.Bayes HC - Wounded
G/9516 Sgt.Bolton H. - Missing.
G/9889 Pte Cooper F. - Wounded
G/9916 " Cullen JH - Wounded
G/9380 Sgt.Campbell CT - Killed
G/9888 Cpl.Cowles G. - Wounded
G/10048 Pte Carel AT - Wounded
G/10411 " Chambers WF - Wounded - To duty
G/10224 Sgt.Chester RC - Died of wounds
G/11012 Pte Campbell WN - Wounded
G/6242 " Cole W. - Wounded
G/25007 " Crow FW - Wounded
G/9822 " Davidson E. - Wounded
G/9826 " Davis WJ. - Wounded
G/6870 " Davis R. - wounded
G/9931 " Drake AH - Killed
G/10044 " Dobie SS - Wounded
G/25019 " Draper T. - Wounded
G/7632 " Ellender H. - Missing.
G/10057 " Elsom AS - Missing.
G/24863 " Evans TH - Wounded
G/9844 L/Cpl.Fendall S. - Killed
G/11264 Pte Fowler W. - Wounded
G/14440 Cpl.Edwards E - Missing.
G/128 Cpl.Gibbons WH - Wounded
G/9800 Pte Hentsch AF - Killed
G/9905 " Huggett AH - Killed
G/6339 " Leader C H Wounded

G/10061 Pte Janes AH - Wounded
G/10389 " Jones AJ. - Wounded
G/10389
G/10363 " Liggins J. - Wounded
G/10050 " Loft GH - Killed..
G/9866 " Leech H. - Wounded
G/7666 " Linkins AL - Wounded
G/10043 " Martin W. - Killed
G/6802 " Mitchell A. - Wounded
G/10382 " Miller H. - Wounded
G/10385 " Matthews S. - Wounded
G/24967 Pte Norris HP - Wounded
G/10407 " Oldfield G. - Wounded
G/9909 " Phillirre PA - Wounded
G/9857 Pte Rourke TJ - Wounded
G/10356 " Readyhoff R. - wounded
G/4635 " Roberts R. - Wounded
G/24544 " Ross C. - Killed.
G/9858 " Scrase W. - Wounded
G/9859 Cpl. Scrase A. - Wounded
G/9856 Pte Swift J. - Wounded
G/9862 " Srink J. - Missing.
G/9896 " Stedman A - Killed
G/9906 L/Cpl.Shepherd J. - Kill
G/9495 Sgt.Saltmarsh FW - Wounded
G/9388 "Saunders W - Wounded
G/10368 Pte Streather F - Wounded
G/10342 Pte Stapleton - died of wounds.
G/10359 Pte Smith T - Killed
G/7326 " Skelton CH - Wounded
G/6598 A/Sgt Stevens AJ - Died of wounds
G/9925 " Turrer A - Wounded
G/9818 " Taylor WH - Wounded
G/9894 " Treadwell H do
G/10395 "Taylor GC do
G/9647 L/Sgt.Taylor JW do
G/10372 Pte Underwood S do
G/10390 " Vickery TV do
G/9824 " Woolnough AW do
G/9864 " Woollett F do
G/9895 Pte Ward GP. do
G/10377 " West AF do
G/10403 " Whitney P. do
G/10375 " Whiting F. do
G/10387 " Wingfield A do
G/10393 " Webb W. do
G/10371 " Wright G. do
G/10354 " Winter JT Slink wound
G/10391 " Timms "

Army Form C. 2118

WAR DIARY
or
INTELLIGENCE SUMMARY
(Erase heading not required.)

OCTOBER
10th Bn "THE QUEENS" R.W. SURREY REGT

Vol 6

349

Place	Date	Hour	Summary of Events and Information	Remarks and references to Appendices
R.R. Ribes	1/10/16		Training	
	2/10/16		move to DERNANCOURT. Inspection by G.O.C. of Transport.	JA
	3/10/16		Trenches taken over POMIERS REDOUBT.	JA
	4/10/16		O.C. 24 Coy Commanders visited future trenches of battalion. (WORCESTER RIFLE & DORSET.) Capt. W.A. POPE wounded.	JA
	5/10/16		moved to Sunken road M35 d 8.8. 4 casualties since dusk yesterday.	JA
	6/10/16		moved to FACTORY TRENCH	JA
	7/10/16		Coys disposed for action. Report of action attached.	JA
	8/10/16		Trenches vacated by 21st K.R.R. taken over	JA
	9/10/16		Above trenches held	JA
	10/10/16		Relieved by Royal Scots Fusiliers relief completed 9.15 pm.	JA
	11/10/16		Battalion moved to BECORDEL via MAMETZ	JA
	12/10/16		BECORDEL training & reorganization	JA
	13/10/16		BECORDEL. Inspection of drafts by G.O.C. move to BUIRE. move completed 4.45.	JA
	14/10/16		BUIRE. training	JA
	15/10/16		BUIRE. G.O.C. 41st Div. presented decorations.	JA
	16/10/16		move to AIRAINES started completed 1.30pm.	JA
	17/10/16		here	JA
	18/10/16		training in AIRAINES.	JA
	19/10/16		move to THIEUSHOUK.	JA
	20/10/16		training in THIEUSHOUK	JA
	21/10/16		move to KENORA CAMP M3C6.5.	JA

WAR DIARY or INTELLIGENCE SUMMARY

OCTOBER Army Form C. 2118.

10th Bn The Queens R^l R^t

Place	Date	Hour	Summary of Events and Information	Remarks and references to Appendices
In the Field	22/10/16		move KENORA CAMP to Trenches from 4/6th Bn. A.I.F. relief complete 6.45 P.M. 1 O.R. wounded.	
	23/10/16		Trenches held	
	24/10/16		— do — — do —	
	25/10/16		— do — — do —	
	26/10/16		— do — — do —	
	27/10/16		— do — — do —	
	28/10/16		Relieved by 32nd R. Fusiliers relief completed 4 pm move to RIDGE WOOD.	
	29/10/16		In Support RIDGE WOOD.	
	30/10/16			
	31/10/16			

Arthur Jarvis, Major
Comdg 10th Bn The Queens
R. W. Surrey Regt.

Confidential

Vol 7

Army Form C. 2118

WAR DIARY or INTELLIGENCE SUMMARY

(Erase heading not required) 1st Bn "THE QUEEN'S" ROYAL WEST SURREY REGT.

NOVEMBER

Place	Date	Hour	Summary of Events and Information	Remarks and references to Appendices
RIDGE WOOD	1/11/16	—	Training &c.	
" "	2/11/16	—	Training &c.	
" "	3/11/16	8·45 p.m.	The Battn. relieved the 32nd Battn. Royal Fusiliers in the trenches – relief completed 10·30 p.m. "C" Coy – Firing Line Trenches M1 – M6; 2 platoons of "D" Coy – Support Trench; 2 platoons "D" Coy – New Reserve Trench; "A" Coy – New Reserve Trench; "B" Coy – in Reserve at Battn. H.Q. Killed No. 10049 a/Sergt. SWANN. &c.	
Trenches	4/11/16	—	Normal &c.	
" "	5/11/16	—	Normal &c.	
" "	6/11/16	—	Normal &c.	
" "	7/11/16	—	Normal &c.	
" "	8/11/16	—	Normal &c.	
" "	9/11/16	—	The Battn. was relieved by the 32nd Bn Royal Fusiliers in the trenches. Relief commenced 2 p.m. & was complete 5·35 p.m. The Bn then marched to LA CLYTTE and encamped in huts. Pte. H. BRAZIER &c. Wounded No. 10498 Pte. R.H. CARR &c. Wounded (while in trenches) No. 21588	
LA CLYTTE	10/11/16	—	Bn employed on working parties in clobor of trenches left yesterday &c.	
" "	11/11/16	—	do —	
" "	12/11/16	—	Bn employed on working parties in trenches &c.	

Army Form C. 2118

WAR DIARY or INTELLIGENCE SUMMARY

(Erase heading not required)

16th Bn "THE QUEENS" R. WEST SURREY. REGT.

Confidential

Instructions regarding War Diaries and Intelligence Summaries are contained in F.S. Regs., Part II. and the Staff Manual respectively. Title Pages will be prepared in manuscript.

Place	Date	Hour	Summary of Events and Information	Remarks and references to Appendices
LA CLYTTE	13/11/16		NOVEMBER	
	14/11/16		Bn employed supplying working parties. Remainder training.	
	15/11/16		do	
Rifle Butts Trenches	16/11/16		Bn relieved 32nd R. Fusiliers in trenches. N18.10 to 7.1. Relief complete 3.35 pm	
	17/11/16		Normal	
	18/11/16		Normal	
	19/11/16		Normal	
	20/11/16		Normal	
	21/11/16		Normal	
RIDGE WOOD	22/11/16		Bn relieved by 32nd R. Fusiliers relief complete 6.15 pm. moved to N13.a Ridge Wood	
	23/11/16		Bn in Support	
	24/11/16		Bn in Support	
	25/11/16		Bn in Support	
	26/11/16		Bn in Support	
Trenches N16.10 - 07.1	27/11/16		Bn relieved the 32nd R. Fusiliers in Right sector Trenches N16.10 - 07.1. relief complete 3.45.	
	28/11/16		Normal. 1 O.R. wounded.	
	29/11/16		Normal. 1 O.R. wounded.	
	30/11/16		Normal. 1 O.R. wounded.	

Talmr James. Lt Col.
Comdg 16th Bn The Queens
R. W. Surrey Regt.

WAR DIARY or INTELLIGENCE SUMMARY

Army Form C. 2118

Vol 8

The Queens Royal West Surrey Regt

DECEMBER

Place	Date	Hour	Summary of Events and Information	Remarks and references to Appendices
Trenches	1/12/16		Relieved by 32nd R Fusiliers. Relief complete 3.50 pm. 2/Lt D.W. JACQUES KILLED	
Lo Clytte	2/12/16		Training working parties	
	3/12/16		— do —	
	4/12/16		— do —	
	5/12/16		— do —	
	6/12/16		— do —	
Trenches	7/12/16		Relief of 32nd R Fusiliers complete 5.10 pm. Trenches N16 c.0 - 0.7	
	8/12/16		Relief of 32nd R Fusiliers	
	9/12/16		Normal	
	10/12/16		Normal. 1 OR killed 3 wounded.	
	11/12/16		Normal	
	12/12/16		Normal	
	13/12/16		Normal	
	14/12/16		Relieved by 32nd R Fusiliers Relief complete 5.50 pm from ridge house 10R killed 1 wounded	
RIDGE WOOD	15/12/16		Normal working parties provided (495)	
	16/12/16		Rest. Enemy raid trenches occupied by 26th R Fusiliers Casualties 1 OR killed 4 OR wounded	
	17/12/16		Normal	

WAR DIARY
or
INTELLIGENCE SUMMARY

Army Form C. 2118

DECEMBER — Queens Regt

Place	Date	Hour	Summary of Events and Information	Remarks and references to Appendices
RIDGE WOOD	19/12/16		NORMAL	
	20/12/16		Battn relieved trenches N18.16 - 07.1 occupied by 3znd R fusiliers. Relief Complete.	
	21/12/16		NORMAL	
	22/12/16		NORMAL	
	23/12/16		NORMAL	
	24/12/16		NORMAL 2/Lt E.H. WOODWARD missing & reported killed on patrol.	
	25/12/16		NORMAL	
	26/12/16		NORMAL	
	27/12/16		Bn relieved by 32nd R fusiliers relief Completed 5.30pm. moved la Clytte	
	28/12/16		Training trenching parties	
	29/12/16		NORMAL	
	30/12/16		NORMAL	
	31/12/16		NORMAL	

R V Seymour Major
for Officer Commanding.

WAR DIARY or INTELLIGENCE SUMMARY

Army Form C. 2118

10th Bn "THE QUEEN'S" R.W. SURREY. REGT.

JANUARY 1917

Vol 9

Place	Date	Hour	Summary of Events and Information	Remarks and references to Appendices
La Clytte Bailleul	1.		Normal	
	2.		Relieved 32nd Royal Fusiliers Trenches N18.10.D.Y.1. Relief Complete 6.25 p.m.	
	3.		Normal	
	4.		Normal 1 O.R. wounded. Right Battn. Headquarters shelled. From letter in 5 Officers wounded Capt F.N.L. Burgess slightly Capt. H.H. Smith 6 O.Rs killed & 12 others wounded emergency headquarters formed & used	
	5.		Right Bn. H.Q. moved to emergency headquarters formed & used	
	6.		Normal	
Ridgewood	7.		Normal	
	8.		Relieved by 32nd Royal Fusiliers & moved to RIDGEWOOD	
	9.		Normal 1/9 at Ridgewood.	
	10.		Normal	
	11.		Normal	
	12.		Normal	
	13.		Normal 1 O.R. wounded.	
	14.		Relieved 32nd Bn. Royal Fusiliers Trenches N18.10.Y.1 Relief complete - 6.10 p.m.	
Trenches	15.		Normal	
	16.		Normal	
	17.		Normal 3/18 reinforced	
	18.		Normal	
	19.		Normal	
	20.		Relieved by 32nd R.F. Relief complete 3.30 p.m. moved to LA CLYTTE	

Army Form C. 2118

WAR DIARY
or
INTELLIGENCE SUMMARY 10th Bn. THE QUEENS R.W. SURREY REGT

(Erase heading not required.)

Instructions regarding War Diaries and Intelligence Summaries are contained in F.S. Regs., Part II. and the Staff Manual respectively. Title Pages will be prepared in manuscript.

Place	Date	Hour	Summary of Events and Information	Remarks and references to Appendices
LACUYTE	21st		TRAINING	
	22nd		do	
	23rd		do	
	24th		do	
	25th		Relieved to 3.5th Bn R. Fusiliers in Trenches N16 n D7¹ Right Coy't H. Sgr A	
	26th		Normal	
TRENCHES	27th		Normal	
	28th		Normal	1 O.R. wounded
	29th		Normal	1 O.R. wounded
	30th		Normal	1 G.R. int... cl...
	31st			

L.S. Andrews Capt + Adjt
10th Bn. "The Queens" Regt.

WAR DIARY
INTELLIGENCE SUMMARY

Army Form C. 2118

10th Bn "THE QUEEN'S" Regt.

FEBRUARY

Place	Date	Hour	Summary of Events and Information	Remarks and references to Appendices
RIDGEWOOD	1/2/17		Bn. relieved by 32nd R. Fusiliers. Relief completed 12 noon. Moved to RIDGEWOOD.	
	2/2/17		Normal.	
	3/2/17		Normal. Lt-Col. R. Oakley, D.S.O., resumed command of Battalion	
	4/2/17		Normal.	
TRENCHES	5/2/17		Bn. relieved 32nd Bn. R. Fusiliers in trenches N18.10 - 07.1 Relief completed 2.30 pm	
	6/2/17		Trench mortars fired on enemy trenches to cut wire. Lt WEBB + 2nd Lt MUIR-SMITH joined for duty	
	7/2/17		Normal in trenches. Battery near B.H.Q shelled for 2½ hours. Ration dump shelled; 3 O.R. wounded.	
	8/2/17		Normal in Bn. sector. Raid by R.W.Kent Regt. on front of Brigade on our left. Successful; 12 prisoners captured.	
	9/2/17		Normal. 1 O.R. killed, 1 wounded	
	10/2/17		Bn. relieved by 22nd R. Fusiliers. moved to La Clytte. 50 O.R. joined	

Army Form C. 2118

WAR DIARY
or
INTELLIGENCE SUMMARY

(Erase heading not required.) 10th Bn. "THE QUEEN'S" Regt.

Instructions regarding War Diaries and Intelligence Summaries are contained in F. S. Regs., Part II. and the Staff Manual respectively. Title Pages will be prepared in manuscript.

FEBRUARY

Place	Date	Hour	Summary of Events and Information	Remarks and references to Appendices
STEENVOORDE	11/2/17		Bn. relieved by 18th K.R.R.C. Moved to STEENVOORDE. Bn. in billets.	
	12/2/17		Training in STEENVOORDE area for a proposed Bn. raid on enemy's line at HOLLANDSCHESCHUUR SALIENT.	
	13/2/17		--- ditto ---	
	14/2/17		--- ditto ---	
	15/2/17		--- ditto ---	
	16/2/17		do	
	17/2/17		do	
	18/2/17		do	
	19/2/17		do	
	20/2/17		do 2 offr. Patrols & parties for duty	
	21/2/17		do " Lynn "	

Army Form C. 2118

WAR DIARY
or
INTELLIGENCE SUMMARY

(Erase heading not required.) 1st Bn THE QUEENS'S REGT

Instructions regarding War Diaries and Intelligence Summaries are contained in F. S. Regs., Part II. and the Staff Manual respectively. Title Pages will be prepared in manuscript.

Place	Date	Hour	Summary of Events and Information	Remarks and references to Appendices
			FEBRUARY	
	22/2/17		Training for Raid continued	
	23/2/17		Move to Mirumbridge Camp.	
Mirumbridge Camp	24/2/17		Raid on Enemy lines at HOLLANDSCHESCHUUR SALIENT carried out. Captain E. BIRD killed 2nd Lt E.H. FAIRCLOUGH died of wounds. Lieut F.J. HONK & 2nd Lt E.H. EDINBOROUGH wounded. O.R. killed 26 wounded 91. missing 11. Prisoners officer 1 & 4 O.R. 1 machine gun captured. Full report attached.	
	25/2/17		Battalion rested in Mirumbridge Camp	
	26/2/17		do	

1875 Wt. W593/826 1,000,000 4/15 J.B.C. & A. A.D.S.S./Forms/C. 2118.

Army Form C. 2118

WAR DIARY
or
INTELLIGENCE SUMMARY

(Erase heading not required.) 10th Bn "The Queens" Regt

FEBRUARY

Place	Date	Hour	Summary of Events and Information	Remarks and references to Appendices
Moulle	27/2/17		Inspection by General Plumer Comdg 2nd Army	
TRENCHES	28/2/17		Bn relieved 32nd R. Fusiliers in trenches, N18,10 - 07.1 Relief Completed 3.45 pm.	

R Oakley Lt Col.
Comdg 10th Bn "The Queens" Regt.

Army Form C. 2118

WAR DIARY
or
INTELLIGENCE SUMMARY

(Erase heading not required.)

10th Bn. THE QUEENS REGT   Vol (XI)

Place	Date	Hour	Summary of Events and Information	Remarks and references to Appendices
Trenches	1/3/17		Normal	
	2/3/17		Normal	
	3/3/17		Normal	
	4/3/17		Normal	
	5/3/17		Normal	
	6/3/17		On relief by 35th R. Fusiliers what completed at 10 pm. Battalion moved to Brigade Reserve at La Clytte	
La Clytte	7/3/17		TRAINING on new organisation	
	8/3/17		TRAINING. With the exception of Lewis Gunners & Signallers all men employed on working parties.	

1875 Wt. W593/826 1,000,000 4/15 J.B.C. & A. A.D.S.S./Forms/C. 2118.

WAR DIARY
or
INTELLIGENCE SUMMARY

Army Form C. 2118

Place	Date	Hour	Summary of Events and Information	Remarks and references to Appendices
In Cl, etc	9/3/17		Training	
	10/3/17		do	
	11/3/17		do	
TRENCHES	12/3/17		Bn relieved the 33rd R. Fusiliers in the Right Subsector N 18, 14 – 07. relief completed 5.20 pm. 1 OR killed	
	13/3/17		Normal	
	14/3/17		Normal	
	15/3/17		Normal	
	16/3/17		Normal	
	17/3/17		Normal	

WAR DIARY
or
INTELLIGENCE SUMMARY

Army Form C. 2118

Place	Date	Hour	Summary of Events and Information	Remarks and references to Appendices
Trenches	18/3/17		Bn relieved by 35th R. Fusiliers relief completed 9.20 am. Moved to RIDGE WOOD. 1 OR wounded.	
RIDGEWOOD	19/3/17		Normal. 2 O.R. wounded.	
	20/3/17		Normal.	
	21/3/17		Battln relieved by 6th Bn North Staffordshire Regt. relief completed 1.30 pm. Bn marched to entrain to STEENVOORDE AREA. arrived 5 pm & debussed to billets.	
STEENVOORDE	22/3/17		Received draft 40 OR Joined.	
	23/3/17		Training. Inspection by General Plumer Comdg 2nd Army.	

Army Form C. 2118

WAR DIARY
or
INTELLIGENCE SUMMARY
(Erase heading not required.)

Instructions regarding War Diaries and Intelligence Summaries are contained in F. S. Regs., Part II. and the Staff Manual respectively. Title Pages will be prepared in manuscript.

Place	Date	Hour	Summary of Events and Information	Remarks and references to Appendices
STEENVOORDE	24/3/17		Training. draft 19 OR joined	
	25/3/17		Training	
	26/3/17		Training	
	27/3/17		Training	
	28/3/17		Training. drafts 1 Offr (off Shute) 31 OR Joined	
	29/3/17		Training	
	30/3/17		Training	
	31/3/17		Training	

P. Mckee Lt Col.
Comdg 10th Bn The Queens Regt

WAR DIARY or INTELLIGENCE SUMMARY

Army Form C. 2118

10th Bn "The Queen's" SURREY REGT. APRIL

Place	Date	Hour	Summary of Events and Information	Remarks and references to Appendices
STEENVOORDE	1/4/17		Presentation of medals by Major General S. Lawford C.B. Comdg 41st Division	
"	2/4/17		Training. Practising the attack	
"	3/4/17		do	
"	4/4/17		do	
"	5/4/17		do	
"	6/4/17		Move to Brigade Reserve at RENINGHELST. Move complete 12.30pm. Battalion accommodated in CHIPPEWA CAMP.	
RENINGHELST	7/4/17		Training. 1 O.R. killed. 2 O.R. wounded	

Army Form C. 2118

WAR DIARY
or
INTELLIGENCE SUMMARY
(Erase heading not required)

10th Bn. "THE QUEENS" R.W. SURREY Regt.   APRIL

Place	Date	Hour	Summary of Events and Information	Remarks and references to Appendices
RENINGHELST	8/4/17		Training	
	9/4/17		Training	
	10/4/17		Training	
	11/4/17		Training	
	12/4/17		Training	
Trenches	13/4/17		Battn relieved the 15th Hampshire Regt & was disposed as under:- Hqr Voormezeele Shut 26 b/shut 6. B Coy less 2 Platoons in VOORMEZEELE SWITCH O 1 to 2.8. to I 31 d 3.4. D Coy in VOORMEZEELE A & C Coy in G.H.Q. 2nd line from H 36 b 7.7. to H 36 d 1/2.6. Remaining 2 Platoons of B Coy in DICKEBUSCH Battn Headquarters in dug-ink at T 31 c 1.6. Orderly Room at DICKEBUSCH. H 26 C 8.1.	

1875 Wt. W593/826 1,000,000 4/15 J.B.C. & A. A.D.S.S./Forms/C. 2118.

Army Form C. 2118

WAR DIARY
or
INTELLIGENCE SUMMARY

(Erase heading not required)

10th Bn "The Queens" W Surrey Regt.   APRIL

Instructions regarding War Diaries and Intelligence Summaries are contained in F.S. Regs., Part II. and the Staff Manual respectively. Title Pages will be prepared in manuscript.

Place	Date	Hour	Summary of Events and Information	Remarks and references to Appendices
Trenches	13/4/17		continued. The Battalion was in support. Relief was completed by 11.50 am.	
	14/4/17		Normal. 1 O.R. wounded. Do	
	15/4/17		Normal. 1 O.R. killed 1 O.R. wounded Do	
	16/4/17		Normal Do	
	17/4/17		Normal Do	
	18/4/17		Normal Do KRR	
	19/4/17		Battn. relieved by 18th Bn Hampshire Regt. Relief completed 11.50 am. Battn. moved to Chippewa Camp.	

Army Form C. 2118

WAR DIARY
or
INTELLIGENCE SUMMARY
(Erase heading not required.)

Instructions regarding War Diaries and Intelligence Summaries are contained in F.S. Regs., Part II. and the Staff Manual respectively. Title Pages will be prepared in manuscript.

Place	Date	Hour	Summary of Events and Information	Remarks and references to Appendices
Cuthbert Camp	20/4/17		Training.	
	21/4/17		Training.	
	22.4.17		Training.	RNG
	23.4.17		Training	RNG
	24.4.17		Battalion relieved the 18th KRR and was disposed as under. Map Voormezeele Sheet 28 SW16. B Coy in Voormezeele Switch Trench. 2 Platoons and Coy Hdqrs O.1.B.2,8 to I.31.d.3.4 and 2 Platoons in VOORMEZEELE. A and C Coys in GHQ advanced line from H.36.b.7,7 to A.33.d.2,6. D Coy in DICKEBUSCHE Batt Hdqrs in dugouts at I.31.C.1,8 orderly Room at DICKEBUSCHE H.28.C.8.1. The Battalion was in Support. Relief was Completed by 11/5 a.m. RNG	
	25.4.17		Normal. RNG	
	26.4.17		Normal RNG	
	27.4.17		Normal RNG	
	28.4.17		Normal RNG	
	29.4.17		Normal RNG	
	30.4.17		Normal RNG	

Strength of Battalion
1. Borne on Books 38 Officers. 950 men
2. Away from Unit 24 Officers 267 men

R Joynerthorpe Lt. Col.

WAR DIARY or INTELLIGENCE SUMMARY

Army Form C. 2118

10th Bn. The Queens Surrey Rgt. Vol 13 MAY

Place	Date	Hour	Summary of Events and Information	Remarks and references to Appendices
Trenches	1.5.17		Normal	
"	2.5.17		Normal	
"	3.5.17		Relieved by 11th Bn. The Queens. Bn. relief complete 11 p.m. & moved to Chippewa Camp. B. Remy Pilot.	
Chippewa Camp	4.5.17 to 10.5.17		Training	
	11.5.17 - 12.5.17		Training. 2 O.R. wounded in working parts	
	7.5.17		Moved to billets near ABEELE (L33 A.S.4) bivouacs	
	12.5.17		Entrained at ABEELE detrained WATTEN marched to billets at BAYENGHEM Sheb 37NE	
Bayenghem	14/5/17 to 30/5/17		Training for attack.	Strength of Battalion on 23.5.17 27 offrs. 809 O.R.

Army Form C. 2118

WAR DIARY
or
INTELLIGENCE SUMMARY

(Erase heading not required)

10th Bn. The Queens (Surrey Rgt.)

MAY

Place	Date	Hour	Summary of Events and Information	Remarks and references to Appendices
	30/5/17		Move to MIDDLE CAMP EAST. (N1 a 5.1.) entrained at WATTEN detrained at ABEELE arrived camp 8.30 am 31st May	
	31/5/17		Rest & working parties.	

Blakey Lt Col.
Comdg 10th Bn The Queens Rgt.

WAR DIARY or INTELLIGENCE SUMMARY

Army Form C. 2118

10th (S) Bn "The Queens" R.W. Surrey

Summary of Events and Information

Strength of Battalion on 1st June 1917 — 39 Officers

Place	Date	Hour	Summary of Events and Information	Remarks and references to Appendices
MIDDLE CAMP EAST	1.6.17		Working and carrying parties	
	4.6.17			
Trenches	5.6.17		Battalion moved to assembly positions. F.L. Trenches. O.1.1 – O.2.1; Reserve Line, G.H.Q Advanced line.	
	6.6.17		Remained in above trenches.	
	7.6.17		Assault on German trenches. See papers attached.	Casualties: 9th March – Wounded 1 Off 3 Off 11 O'Ranks 56 O'Ranks
	8.6.17		Relieved by 9th Buffs and moved to Ridgewood.	
	9.6.17 10.6.17		Remained in fields near Ridgewood.	
	11.6.17		Relieved 9th Essex Regt in line Relief complete 12 midnight Trenches N E Bonnet Rose Wood - Ravene Wood - Clive Trench	
	12.6.17 13.6.17		Trenches held. Abnormal shelling of front + support lines	Killed – Wounded 1 Off
	14.6.17		Attack by 122nd Bde on left. 4th objective successfully taken and held. Heavy retaliation by the enemy into Ravene & Denys Woods	17 O'Rks 4 O'Ranks
	15/16.6.17		Trenches held	2 Offs 7 O'Ranks 9 O'Rks
	17.6.17		Relieved by 3rd Bn The Royal Fusiliers. Moved to trenches round the Dammstrasse	

Army Form C. 2118

WAR DIARY
or
INTELLIGENCE SUMMARY
(Erase heading not required.)

10th Bn "The Queens" R.W.S. Regt.

Place	Date	Hour	Summary of Events and Information	Remarks and references to Appendices
				Casualties
				Killed / Wounded
	18/21.6.19		In above positions	
	22.6.19		Relieved 26th Bn Royal Fusiliers in left sector. Ottawa trench in Ravine Wood - Shellbeke Rd.	7 O.Ranks / 1 Off
	23/26.6.19		Above trenches held.	8 O.Ranks / 19 O.Ranks
	27.6.19		Relieved by 32nd Bn Royal Fusiliers. Moved to Bois Confluent. Relief complete 3.30am	
	28.6.19		Remained in Bde Reserve.	
	29.6.19		Moved to Reninghelst having been relieved by 22nd Londons Regt.	
	30.6.19		Marched to Blévin training area. Battalion in Billets & tents.	

Strength of Battalion 30th June 1919 - 29 Officers 816 O.Ranks

Shyne Major
Comdg 10th The Queens Regt

Headquarters,

   124th. Infantry Brigade.

      With reference to the action of the 7th. June 1917, I beg to report that :-

(1) The concentration previous to the battle was well carried out and the final move of the Battalion to their assembly positions in "NO MAN'S LAND" and in rear of our trenches was carried out without hitch.
As it was nearly a full moon I had gaps cut in our front line parapet to enable the leading assaulting Companies to get out without being seen over the top; but even then many men when the time for getting out into NO MANS LAND came, insisted on calmly walking over the skyline.
I think this was seen by the enemy and I am quite certain that they did see the battalion on my left as some quarter of an hour before ZERO they put up a number of golden rain rockets evidently calling for artillery support but luckily nothing followed except a few shells over the Battalion on my left.

(2) The men of the battalion true to the characteristics of the British Soldier went to sleep in their assembly positions when waiting for ZERO. The explosion of the mines however, under the ST. ELOI craters woke them up and the whole Battalion, in the formation under which they had been trained advanced to the assault.

(3) The capture of the front line system presented no difficulties and we assembled on the Red Line in rear of OATEN WOOD.
The remainder of the advance was carried out by Companies according to programme and we finally established ourselves on the Black Line our final objective in accordance with the time table.

(4) The following points may be of interest. The wonderful value of the previous training and the surprising intelligence shown by all ranks which contributed very largely to our success. I mean that nearly all throughout the day seemed to know where they were and what they were up to.
I think that Zero Hour was ten minutes too early as it was very dark when we first started off and the difficulty of maintaining direction before daylight came was very great.
Previous to our advance from the OATEN WOOD line, myself and Adjutant who were luckily up with the leading Company saw to our horror a Battalion apparently in fours advancing in our immediate rear. Some of their Companies insisted in moving right over to our left flank and had entirely lost themselves. This was exceedingly awkward for us as they were the Battalion of the 56th. Infantry Brigade detailed to carry on the attack in conjunction with my right for the assault on the next objective. We got the North Staffs into position and all went well.
I cannot speak too highly of the Artillery Barrage and it was entirely due to them that we were able to carry out such a long advance without serious loss.
Remarkably few enemy dead or wounded were seen lying about and either the then trench systems were very lightly

P.T.O.

held or large numbers had been buried by our shell fire.
　　　　The Battalion captured five machine guns but I am not certain of the number of prisoners.
　　Our total casualties were :

	Officers	Other Ranks
Killed	1	6
Missing		13
Wounded	3	33
Wounded & Missing		1

The Battalion went into action;

Officers	Other Ranks
16	610

　　　　　　　　　　　　　　　Rakii　　Lt. Col.

10/6/17　　　　　　　　　　20th. Bn. "The Queen's" R.W.S.Regt.

Copy No 8

Operation Orders by	No. 52.
Major R.V. Gwynne. D.S.O.	B.E.F.
Comdg. "The Queens" Regt.	28.6.17.

No.	Subject.

1. The Battalion will be relieved by the 22nd Bn. London Regt. on the night 29/30th June commencing about 7 pm.

2. On completion of relief, Companies will proceed to ALBERTA CAMP, RENINGHELST via Overland Track. Movement will be by platoons at 100 yards distance.

3. Officers Kits, cooking utensils, mess baskets etc., will be carried to the point where the Overland Track cuts the Reserve Line, i.e. "C" Company Headquarters by 6 pm.
Transport Officer will arrange necessary transport. Officers chargers will be on the Overland Track by GORDON FARM at ~~9.00~~ 7.30 pm.

4. On 30th June the Battalion will march to training area near METEREN at X 10 c 5¼ (Sheet 27 S.E.). March Orders will be issued later. Time of departure about 5.30pm. Transport will accompany the Battalion.

5. The attention of Company Commanders and Transport Officer is called to the necessity of leaving the areas in a clean condition, and certificates will be obtained from Coy. Commanders and T.O. of opposite numbers to this effect. These certificates will be forwarded to Orderly Room on arrival at METEREN.

6. Completion of relief will be reported as soon as possible to B.H.Q. by runner.

7. ACKNOWLEDGE.

[signature]
Capt & Adjt.
"The Queens" RWS Regt.

```
Copy No.  1 to Commanding Officer.
  "   "   2     File.
  "   "   3     O.C. "A" Coy.
  "   "   4     O.C. "B" Coy.
  "   "   5     O.C. "C" Coy.
  "   "   6     O.C. "D" Coy.
  "   "   7     Transport Officer & Quartermaster.
  "   "   8     War Diary.
  "   "   9     22nd Bn. London Regt.
  "   "  10     R.S.M.
```

WO 4/633
Army Form C. 2118

WAR DIARY
or
INTELLIGENCE SUMMARY

(Erase heading not required.) 10th Bn. The Queens R.W. Surrey Regt.

Month July 1917

Instructions regarding War Diaries and Intelligence Summaries are contained in F.S. Regs., Part II. and the Staff Manual respectively. Title Pages will be prepared in manuscript.

Place	Date	Hour	Summary of Events and Information	Remarks and references to Appendices
METEREN	1/7/17		The battalion was employed in billets and took in training.	
	16/7/17		Carried out including practice attack on enemy positions. Draft of about 132 OR arrived on 15th-17th	
	17/7/17		B & C Coys ordered up to RIDGE WOOD (N.5 central) to assist 32nd Bn R Fusiliers in supplying working parties	
WESTOUTRE	18/7/17		Battalion, less B & C Coys, moved to WESTOUTRE and in camp at N6.c.1.4.	
	19/7/17 - 24/7/17		Training practice in the attack. War Establishment 608 wounded	
LA CLYTTE	25/7/17		Battalion less B & C Coys moved to DE ZON Camp M.13.c.9.3. B & C Coys rejoined from RIDGE WOOD	

Army Form C. 2118

WAR DIARY
or
INTELLIGENCE SUMMARY
(Erase heading not required.)

Place	Date	Hour	Summary of Events and Information	Remarks and references to Appendices
DE ZON Camp	26/7/17 — 29/7/17		Training carried out with a view to the attack LSS	
	30/7/17		Battalion moved to assembly position at VOORMEZEELE	
	31/7/17		Battalion moved to support of 123rd Infantry Brigade and accommodated in Bluff tunnels I 34 C II	
			Strength of Battalion 31 Officers 950 OR	

Wensley Dott
Lt Col
Commanding the Queen's Rgt.

WAR DIARY or INTELLIGENCE SUMMARY

Army Form C. 2118

10 R W Surrey Regt
August 1916

Place	Date	Hour	Summary of Events and Information	Remarks and references to Appendices
TRENCHES	2/5/16		The Battalion was ordered to move from BLUFF TUNNELS at 1.30 a.m. and to advance to the Red Line to show it up. B & C Coys to hop up between Red & Blue lines at 3.10 a.m. At 4.30 a.m. A & D Coys would pass through B & C Coys and capture, hold the spur of the hill approx. Green line. One guide only was provided for the whole of the Battalion, neither any of the Officers or men had ever been over the ground before and the guide lost his way. Zero hour for the operation was 4.30 a.m. the leading companies of the Battalion (C Coy) reached the Red line at 4.30 a.m. whereas it should have mopped up between Red & Blue line. At 3.10 a.m. near the column was heavily shelled and Capt. H.C. Hilder Leven was first wounded then killed, A Coy now & being shell fire and casualties became somewhat disorganised and reached BATTLE WOOD 50 men strong under 2nd/Lt. Parks. Had forward at 4.30 a.m. 2 remnants	

Army Form C. 2118

WAR DIARY
or
INTELLIGENCE SUMMARY
(Erase heading not required.)

Page 2

Place	Date	Hour	Summary of Events and Information	Remarks and references to Appendices
	1st August		the position & ascertain whether it would be possible to attack what had the enemy barrage all the advantage of which had it come, been lost by the time. It was twice hit in the thigh by machine gun bullets and after some time was brought in by stretcher-bearers. Any movement in 2 guards O6.a.16 was impossible owing to fire from machine guns located in dug-outs at O6.d.1.6. At 7am the disposition of the battalion was as follows C Coy. in dug-outs and still held. along E side of Railway embanked about O6.a.4.2. to O6.a.3.1. B 1 D Coy along W side of Railway from O6.a.3.4. to 136.c.1.6. A Coy in BATTLE WOOD about 1.35.c.y.6. and it remained the same until nightfall. Major J.L. Andrew took over command of the battalion at 1.30pm having been ordered up from detail.	

WAR DIARY or INTELLIGENCE SUMMARY

Army Form C. 2118

App 3

Place	Date	Hour	Summary of Events and Information	Remarks and references to Appendices
	3rd August		An into Brigade Relief between 1/23rd Rifle & 1/4th Bde was proceeded by carried out about 10 pm. No guides were provided by H.Q. the Queens R(?) which was our opposite number and they of course only had vague ideas as to the position of their men. Eventually a line was decided on (shown on map "B") and this was held as an outpost line owing to the state of the ground it was impossible to dig a continuous line. This relief was completed by 11 pm. It is impossible to estimate the casualties for the operation owing to the number of men who lost themselves and afterwards reported that it was by seen by operation orders "attached" that it was hoped if certain circumstances arose to advance and capture the LANDVOORDE line. Unfortunately the was not possible. The attack on the Green line which should have been carried out by 1/23rd Bn 4th Bde. and was afterwards allotted	

WAR DIARY
or
INTELLIGENCE SUMMARY

(Erase heading not required.)

Army Form C. 2118

Place	Date	Hour	Summary of Events and Information	Remarks and references to Appendices
	1st August		to find Bn. H.Q. was not a real success owing to the fact that only one guide was provided with his also to three reached from the last was. also to three reached from the last afterwards located at O.6.d.7.5. and which had apparently been overlooked by the Intelligence Corps and the heavy artillery. The weather on the subsequent days was the worst imaginable the ground became so bad that some of the men who fell into shell holes died from exhaustion before they [could] be extracted. Orders & maps attacked.	Page 4 [?]
	2nd August		Fairly quiet day. Night continuous rain.	
	3rd August		The battalion was ordered to relieve the 23rd Bn. The Middlesex Regt. in day posts and outposts along E side of the Railway Embankment. Reliefs was completed at 11 pm and the battalion frontage then extended from O.6.c.4.4 to	

WAR DIARY or INTELLIGENCE SUMMARY

Army Form C. 2118

page 5

Place	Date	Hour	Summary of Events and Information	Remarks and references to Appendices
Dunelm	Aug 3rd		O6 c 44 to O6 b 30 90... a frontage of one hoo yards. Owed to the war red and harsh nature of the ground it was needed to kill the lane there as an outpost line and to cover the front with machine gun and rifle fire from the Railway Embankment and the ground right up to the dugouts at O6 d 7.8. The disposition of the battalion was as follows - A travel by troop to O6 a + b. 1 line from 3 two hr... aloof E ride of Railway Embankment 3 line for so a.c. Lateral post face and ad each night fire the two positions to the Blue line. The enemy occupied the dug-out at O6 d 7.8 and the ruins howls at O6 d 0.6. The remainder of the battalion was aloof the W side of the Embankment there e continuous travel was dug. Batt HQ was at O6 a 4.4. 32nd Royal Fusiliers left where 5/4th KRRC Man left by Capt Bessant.	

Army Form C. 2118

WAR DIARY
or
INTELLIGENCE SUMMARY
(Erase heading not required.)

page 6

Place	Date	Hour	Summary of Events and Information	Remarks and references to Appendices
Iresbles	Aug 3rd		in a dug-out in the Rly. Embankment (the firing was taking towards to the front line)	
	Aug 4th		Heavily shelled all day, counter attack by enemy on HOUTHEKE. and also on P.O. on our left, enemy penetrated at both places but was driven out by the morning. Proportions as above except A Coy was sent back to BATTLE WOOD at I 35 c.7.6	
	Aug 5th		Heavily shelled all day at about 9.30 p.m. enemy SOS attacks at HOUTHEKE on both sides artillery & machine gun fire. No enemy were seen attacking on our front and it as they attacked a bat flank it would seem that they were held up by our artillery and machine gun fire. Seven casualties	

WAR DIARY or **INTELLIGENCE SUMMARY**
(Erase heading not required.)

Army Form C. 2118

page 4

Place	Date	Hour	Summary of Events and Information	Remarks and references to Appendices
Trenches H36 c 3.4.	Aug 7th		Quiet day. Relieved at night by 23rd the Middlesex Rgt. Relief completed by 2 am. Bn moved to camp at H36 c 3.4. The Battalion went into action 19 Officers 585 O.R. strong and during the period 1st – 6th inclusive sustained the following casualties. KILLED. A/Capt H.C. WILSONS-LEWIS. 27 other Ranks. WOUNDED. A/Lt. Col. R.V. GWYNNE. DSO. 2nd Lt. R.C. WILSON. – Lt. WILLS. (at duty) 130 other Ranks. MISSING. 5 " "	Yes Yes Yes
H 36 c 3.4.	Aug 7th		A/Lt. Col. F. HAZLEY BELL took over command of the Battalion.	Yes
H W35 c 7/4	Aug 8th to Aug 10th		Moved to camp at H 35 c 7.4. Bn rested and reorganized. Details were added to the strength. Camp Etc	

WAR DIARY or INTELLIGENCE SUMMARY

Army Form C. 2118

page 8

Place	Date	Hour	Summary of Events and Information	Remarks and references to Appendices
Trenches	Aug 12th		Battalion relieved the 11th Bn The Queen's Regt as battalion in Brigade reserve to Left Brigade. Disposed as follows A & C Coys. RAVINE WOOD. 1 & 3 C B.HR.; B & D Coys. ECLUSE TRENCH. O 3.b.	
	Aug 13th		Normal	
	Aug 13th		A & C Coys moved back to ECLUSE TRENCH 2 O.R. wounded by far shelling from 12.30 am - 1.45 am	
	Aug 14th		Normal, except for far shelling from 12.30 am - 1.45 am	
	Aug 15th		Battalion relieved by 5th Bn Rifle Brigade. Relief completed at 6 am. Moved back to WILTSHIRE Fm. and then at 4 pm entrained at HALLEBAST CORNER HILL & 807 and moved to TWEEHOEK AREA where the Battalion was disposed in Bivouac Huts. O 20 d & J 14.	

WAR DIARY or INTELLIGENCE SUMMARY

Army Form C. 2118

page 1.

Place	Date	Hour	Summary of Events and Information	Remarks and references to Appendices
THIELSHOEK	16th -18th		Training & reorganization. At 9.45 p.m. on the 17th a hostile plane dropped a bomb at the middle of the camp & caused the following casualties:— Officers 1 wounded O.R. 36 killed 7 Sgts 1 wounded 61 wounded. There were no lights in camp at the time and the majority of the men were killed by the tent ropes in their tent ropes. In addition to have a little of the pasture of the French horse companies were herded together & occupied space & in consequence the men were asleep in the tents the ??? previously been asked to use of the whole field for the camp but has been refused on the ground of damage to pasture. The men were bored in a square of the site of the space cleared of anythere by the fire. Reference S 39 a 9.4.	

Army Form C. 2118

WAR DIARY
or
INTELLIGENCE SUMMARY
(Erase heading not required.)

Page 10

Place	Date	Hour	Summary of Events and Information	Remarks and references to Appendices
Thouroult	Aug 19th		Funeral service for men killed by bomb.	
	Aug 20th – 24th		Training. Inspection by General's Plumer, Morland and Rawlinson.	
STAPLE	Aug 25th		Battalion moved to STAPLE en route for St OMER. R.33.c.d.d. I was trained will.	
ST MARTINS to LAERI	Aug 3th		Battalion moved to St MARTINS billeted in the village	
	Aug 31st	3.0	Trained. Inspection 3.00 by Field Marshal Sir Douglas Haig K.T. etc	J. Hayley Ell. Lt.Col. Comd. 70th Bn. The Queen's R.

Army Form C. 2118

WAR DIARY
or
INTELLIGENCE SUMMARY (1)
(Erase heading not required.)

1st Queens R.W. Surrey Regt.

Vol 17

Place	Date	Hour	Summary of Events and Information	Remarks and references to Appendices
ST MARTINS AU-LAERT	1st Sept 2nd-5th		Training - Presentation of medal ribbons by Divisional Commander. Do	
	6th		Recd. Warning Ordrs for attack on TOWER HAMLETS RIDGE (J.27 a central)	
	7th		Practised attack on marked out model of German position	
	8th		Do do + a barrage represented by flags	
	9th		Do do	
	10th		Training - Running Range. Conjunction with the rest of the Division.	
	12th		Practice of G. Inst.	
	13th & 14th		Recd. Op. Orders from Bde. Training	
ST MARIE CAPELLE 15th/16th	15th		Rest. Bn marched to ST MARIE CAPELLE (billets now stayed night in billets)	
THIEUSHOUK RIDGE WOOD	17th		" " THIEUSHOEK and stayed the night in huts	
	18th		" " RIDGE WOOD area near DICKEBUSCH. Spent night in huts	
	19th		Fitted out with bombs + extra ammunition - two days rations - and marched to the following positions where we spent the night. A + B coys in CANADA TUNNEL B+D in ECLUS TUNNEL	
	20th		Under cover of darkness the Bn moved up to its assembly position - a taped out line running N-S from J 25 b 3.6½ — J 25 b 2½.4½. A few casualties from shelling in so doing. Our objective was :- A + B coys. the red line 12 about N.S. just E of JAVA ave. D of JAVA tunnel + JAVA drive	

1875 Wt. W593/826 1,000,000 4/15 T.B.C. & A. A.D.S.S./Forms/C. 2118.

WAR DIARY or INTELLIGENCE SUMMARY

(2) 10th Queens R.W. Surrey Regt

Place	Date	Hour	Summary of Events and Information	Remarks and references to Appendices
	20/9		J.26.a.6.6 — J.26.a.6.0. On the taking of this B+D Coys were to pass through A+C and take the blue line ie approx N+S from about J.26.b.2.5 — J.26.b.2.8. On this being taken the 32nd R Fusiliers were to pass through us & take the green line ie the part of TOWER HAMLETS RIDGE. The whole area was subjected to inthst bombardment for several days prior to the attack. At zero hour 5.40 a.m. the Bn, followed immediately in its rear by 32 R Fus, advanced in unison close behind its own very light barrage. The german barrage was met with in addition to very heavy machine gun fire which did great havoc. intirely away its officers. Maj. ANDREWS (who was commanding the Bn.) & Lieuts A.J. Hives & M.T.Nau killed. 2/Lts HARE and TOOMBS TROMBS with Sgt BUSBY were able to keep some men together & succeeded in working round some machine gun positions killing the crew. They were subsequently enforced back. Very disorganised, both its objectives in spite of	

WAR DIARY
or
INTELLIGENCE SUMMARY.
(Erase heading not required.)

Army Form C. 2118.

(3) 10th Queens R.W. Surry Regt

Place	Date	Hour	Summary of Events and Information	Remarks and references to Appendices
	20.		heavy machine gun fire. Capt. J. Willis Hart, M.C. being wounded in the back & command of the Bn. which he managed. We then dug in. During the day the Germans subjected our B. line position to intermittent shelling	
	21.	2pm	from about 2pm till 7pm the Germans bombarded our position very heavily	
		3pm		
		7pm	Intensity of the rifle fire eased to end. At 7 pm the Germans attacked to stop shelling but were completely repulsed by our artillery & rifle fire.	
	22.		Our position was in Battalion front during the day, most difficult was to enforce r ration & water to other in trench with no horses for any to surface r M. gun fire etc. In the same reasons men suffered from a lack of sufficient food & water. HeadQuarters 22/23 half the Bn. was relieved by the Cambs Cyclist Regt. and proceeded to RIDGE WOOD area N water	
	23.		Cambridge Cyclists, M.G. five battery - No rations arrived for the remainder of the Bn. Motor Bn. were relieved the following day & marched at OUDERDOM/ZESTEIN and approx	
PRADELLES	24.		At about 5 am the remainder of Bn. were relieved by and marched to PRADELLES	
	25.		moved to RIDGE WOOD AREA where they entrained for PRADELLES	

Army Form C. 2118.

WAR DIARY
or
INTELLIGENCE SUMMARY.
(Erase heading not required.)

Instructions regarding War Diaries and Intelligence Summaries are contained in F.S. Regs., Part II. and the Staff Manual respectively. Title pages will be prepared in manuscript.

10th Queens R.W. Surrey Regt

Place	Date	Hour	Summary of Events and Information	Remarks and references to Appendices
PRADELLES	25th		Wipers Fund raised £20000 (from 26th R.F.) 6 Officers + 121 other ranks	
	26.27th		Dismounted Journey (14 Survey) moved on a draft to reinforcement Camp.	
			+ 150 from 2/5 Buffs. As reorganisation + reequipment noted In. by 9 OC. Bde.	
CHYVELDE	28th		Bn moved by Bus to CHYVELDE.	
	29th		Bde. "Reorganisation" carried out. To find escorts by aircraft men	
			employed in scavenging work	
			Lt. Col. Hughy Bell resumed command. Major Hanger 2nd in Command.	
	30th		190 men coming from 2/5 Buffs.	
			Effective strength at beginning of month 38 officers Offrs. Other ranks at end of Month 27 Offrs	
			S/C. O. Ranks WK	747, 928

Hughy Bell
Lt. Col.

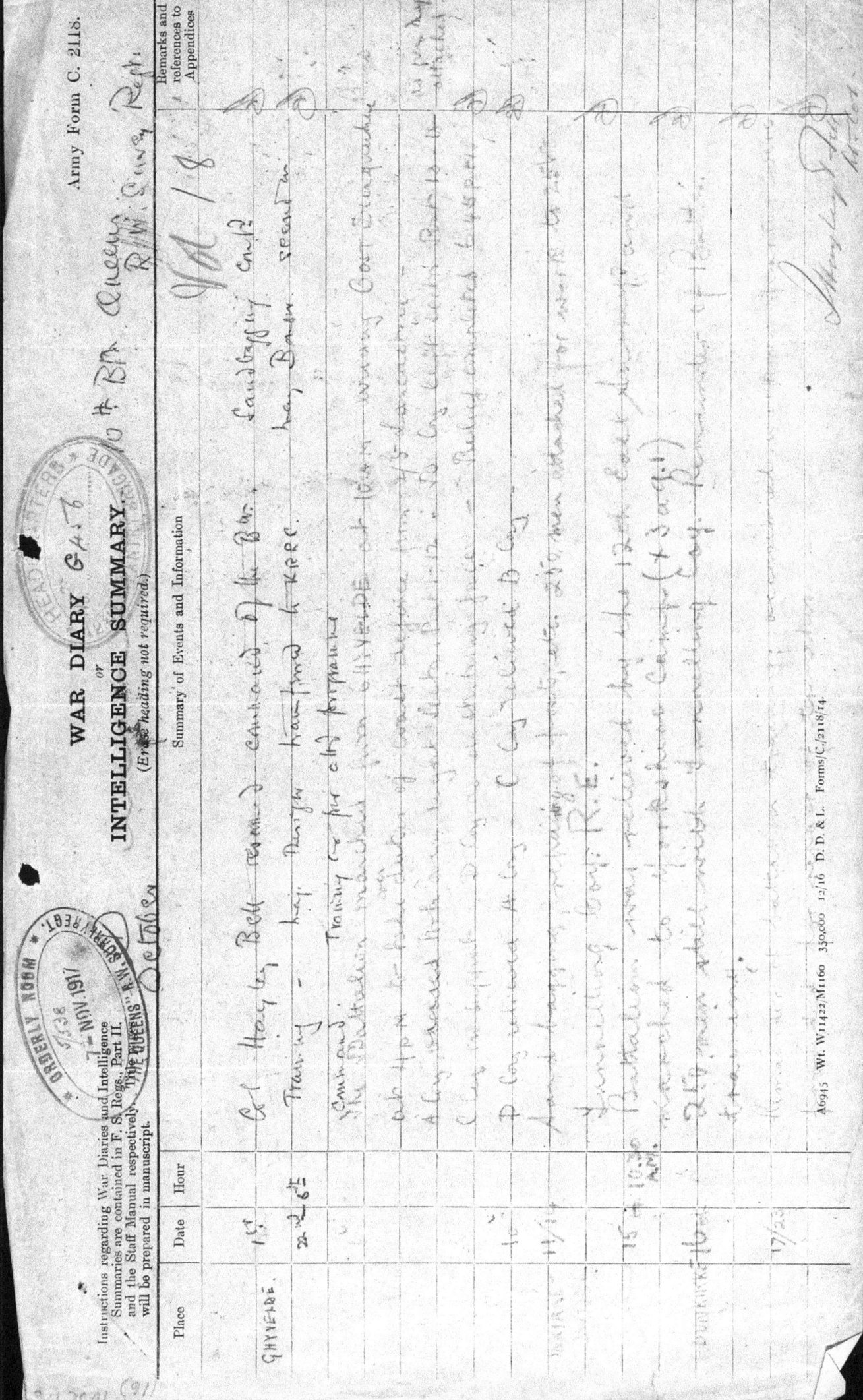

Army Form C. 2118.

WAR DIARY or INTELLIGENCE SUMMARY.

(Erase heading not required.)

OCTOBER — 10th Queens P.W. Surry Regt.

Place	Date	Hour	Summary of Events and Information	Remarks and references to Appendices
	25/27		10 W of 32nd Corps Infantry Right Batt. Interpreter	
	24-29		Holding line. Slight shelling by enemy, otherwise very quiet. Three casualties.	
	29/29 Mid-night		Relieved by 7th Black Watch. Battalion transported to St. Jdéabalde where it embussed at about 5.30 am 29th inst + proceeded to billets at UXEM	
	30/31st		Training	

Douglas Bell
Lt Col

www.ingramcontent.com/pod-product-compliance
Lightning Source LLC
Chambersburg PA
CBHW081553160426
43191CB00011B/1916